MICHAEL BROADBENT'S
· POCKET GUIDE TO ·
WINETASTING

HOW TO APPROACH AND APPRECIATE WINE

MITCHELL BEAZLEY
IN ASSOCIATION WITH
CHRISTIE'S WINE PUBLICATIONS

Michael Broadbent's Pocket Guide to Winetasting

First published in Great Britain in 1982
by Mitchell Beazley,
an imprint of Reed Consumer Books Limited
Michelin House, 81 Fulham Road
London SW3 6RB
and Auckland, Melbourne, Singapore and Toronto

Commissioning Editor Sue Jamieson
Editor Lucy Bridgers
Designer Paul Drayson
Production Controller Juliette Butler

A CIP catalogue record for this book is available from the
British Library
ISBN 1 85732 761 6

Typeset by Service Filmsetting Ltd, Manchester, England
Produced by Mandarin Offset
Printed in Malaysia

CONTENTS

PREFACE

I was convinced forty years ago – and the conviction remains to this day – that in wine tasting and wine-talk there is an enormous amount of humbug.

T. G. Shaw
Wine, the Vine and the Cellar, 1863

Perhaps I should explain that I am a wine merchant by training and a wine auctioneer by profession; and in both capacities I have had constant dealings with that most important of all beings, the consumer. Not being a scientist, an oenologist, a planter of vines or a maker of wine, my viewpoint is based fair and square on the finished product, as it appears on the market, in the cellar and on the table. I have also been actively concerned with wine trade education since the early 1960s and, through lecturing – almost always in the form of what are now known as 'tutored tastings' with interested amateur audiences – for some thirty years.

This work on tasting began life as a slim pamphlet, *Notes on the Techniques of Tasting*, written as a training manual for Harvey's staff in Bristol. It was conceived because of the realization that, asked to judge a wine, most people did not have the foggiest idea what to look for. It seemed to me at the time that a basic and methodical approach was called for; and I have never had good reason to change my mind.

Shortly after, this basic work was serialized in a trade journal, then in *Wine* magazine, whose revered editor, Kathleen Bourke, encouraged me to expand it and have it put out in book form. *Wine Tasting* was first published in 1968 and has been through about ten editions, not to mention several in foreign languages. Each edition has been revised, sometimes expanded, in the light of further experience, much of which was based on the feed-back from my tasting audiences. And one learns from wine itself. Indeed, I usually preface my remarks by saying that the wine is doing all the talking and I am merely trying to translate.

The important point to bear in mind is that there is a reason for every colour, smell and taste. Every facet of a wine's effect on our senses, particularly of sight, smell and taste, is meaningful. Exploring and understanding these facets help us to appreciate a wine more fully; recognizing them will enable us to identify its origin and type.

You do not need to be an expert, or even particularly interested in wine, in order to enjoy drinking it. But tasting is not the same as drinking. Drinking pleases, mellows, loosens the tongue and inhibitions; drinking wine with food is healthy and natural; drinking good wine with good food in good company is one of life's most civilized pleasures. To some, tasting is work, tasting is learning; tasting adds immeasurably to understanding, and, understanding to deeper enjoyment.

The following chapters are ambitiously directed at both the beginner and the more experienced taster, to awaken interest and to encourage even hard-nosed professionals to think more carefully about the methods and words they use. Above all, as I wrote in the first edition, I aim to encourage those teetering on the brink to plunge into the unfathomable depths of wine.

I
THE APPROACH TO TASTING

The difference in a trial of wine by the consumer and the expert, is that the former seeks for something agreeable, something to praise; whilst the latter seeks for a fault, a blemish, or something to condemn.
Arpad Haraszthy
Wines and Vines of California, 1889

It is not necessary to know all about the internal combustion engine in order to drive a car. It is, however, generally agreed that driving lessons are essential and, in the final analysis, practice makes perfect. In the same way, a detailed knowledge of viniculture and viticulture is not a prerequisite for the enjoyment of wine, though an understanding of basic principles, some experience and a fairly discerning palate are essential if wine is to be appreciated as something more than just an ordinary drink.

Ability to taste

If one can taste food, one can taste wine. Generally speaking what *is* good smells and tastes good; what smells 'off' and has a nasty taste is bad. I believe this is the reason why most people are able, correctly, to judge that one wine is better than another simply on the basis that it tastes or smells nicer: that elementary hedonistic judgment will fairly accurately pin down the relative quality of the wines in question. Saying *why* one is better than another is a different matter. There are, however, exceptions to the above rule: an overmature wine, like an overripe cheese or well-hung game bird, sometimes has a putrid overtone to the smell and taste which can be unattractive, even repellent, to the uninitiated, though appreciated, sometimes sought after, by a connoisseur. It is all a matter of taste, *and* experience. Experience, as always, takes time; it cannot be bought or swotted up.

First principles

But what about the first principles? Of all the books, articles and spoken words on the subject of wine, how many describe what the wine actually tastes like or indeed how to set about tasting it? In the course of some pretty voracious reading, up to the time I originally wrote this work, I had come across not a book, hardly a chapter, which dealt with what I considered a fairly basic subject: taste. This is not to say that background information about districts, soil, grape varieties, wine-making and wine-makers is not interesting or valuable; indeed, later chapters deal with the influence of such elements on taste. The history of wine, of firms and people, add to one's awareness, but such vital fringe activities are apt to obscure the main object of the exercise which is the appreciation of wine: its colour, bouquet and flavour. Over the past few years there has been a positive spate of attempts, more and less successful, to deal with the subject. The French, in particular, seem to be making up for lost time (as witnessed by the number of books listed in the Appendix).

There are, of course, difficulties in getting down to brass tacks. Tasting is subjective, and the language needed for describing wine smells and flavours is still singularly ill-defined and anything but universally accepted. What perhaps is needed is something approaching musical notation, for in many ways the problems are similar. Both music and wine appeal to the senses; both are fleeting, in the sense that actual sounds and flavours cannot be retained by the receptive ear or palate; both, on the other hand, can be appreciated, even greatly loved, by those who lack technical knowledge or who are without a deep interest. But to reach the heights of full understanding and to convey this to others rather more is required.

The first stage is an awareness of first principles; the second is a detailed understanding of what lies behind the colour, smell and taste of any wine; and the third is plenty of practice.

Practice, memory and notes

Although wine can be consumed with enjoyment without a lot of fuss and nonsense, reasoned judgment of the finer wines must be based on knowledge, and this can only be acquired by the sort of practice in tasting that will help a vinous memory – a memory that will hold in store the great touchstones, the standard norms and the exceptions to the rules.

There is no doubt that some people are endowed with a more delicate and sensitive palate than others, but this alone is less useful than a normal but well-trained and experienced palate. Mind you, a refined palate *and* an excellent memory will give a relatively new taster a head start. The greatest tasters will surely be those with all the physical attributes, wide experience and a flawless memory. In the end it is almost always memory which lets one down, which is why it is advisable to makes notes – a subject dealt with at length in Chapters VIII and IX.

Perspective and common sense

The important thing is to keep tasting in perspective, to spend time and effort only on those wines that are worthy of attention, and to talk intensely about wine only with those who are of like mind. In short, don't get carried away; use a little common sense.

NEED TO TASTE?

In passing the lips, crossing the tongue and descending the throat, wine is to some extent tasted, whether or not a comment or judgment is made. However, the word 'tasting' in relation to wine refers to a deliberate, conscious and subjective act, the object of which is to assess the qualities of the wine under review. Incidentally, the word 'tasting' is used here (as the French use *dégustation*) in the broader conventional sense, which I prefer to the more academic terms 'sensory' and 'organoleptic' examination.

Does *all* wine need to be tasted in this sense? The answer is no. For of the millions of gallons produced and marketed, by far the largest proportion is the plainest of ordinary beverage wine, made to be consumed as an adequate accompaniment to a meal or merely as a refreshing drink. This sort of wine is *not* intended to be sipped reverently; nor is it meant to provide the basis of intellectual discussion. It is immaterial that one of the end products of its consumption may be the mellowing of the drinkers and loosening of their tongues to discuss *other* subjects with new enlightenment. Ordinary wine is for talking over, not talking about.

Before finally dismissing plain, honest-to-goodness (one

hopes) *vin de table*, a word about mass-produced wines may not come amiss.

Oenology, commerce and mediocrity

We are living in a world where, whether we like it or not, standards are concertinaing. Thanks to new pesticides, new methods of controlling fermentation and other new techniques, less is now left to chance. Although fine vintages cannot be created artificially, certainly poor vintages are less disastrous than they used to be. This is a mixed blessing. If oenologists can rightly take credit for much of the improvement in the overall standard of wine-making, they are also answerable for some of the decrease in character and individuality of fine wines in certain classic areas. If more sound wine is made, then more is to be marketed; and the production of wine is as subject to the law of supply and demand as any other commodity.

It is no coincidence that we live in the era of the 'light' and 'mild', subjected to a relatively new set of standards which applies to nearly all consumer products from mild-flavoured cornflakes to light whiskies. Unhappily, commercial necessity forces this pace, taking character and stuffing out of the raw material, reducing the awareness of the consumer to any elements of positive taste. What is not sufficiently realized is that mixing individual flavours can have a similar effect to mixing colours: the more they are mixed, the greyer the result.

Mass-marketed wines have to be blended. Blended wines, of necessity and by design, lose much of their individuality and character and a 'grey' neutral wine often results. Neutral wines are inoffensive and therefore will not displease the majority. Which, unfortunately, is just one more example of how commercial necessity can become a marketing virtue.

Vital critical standards

It is in the context of maintaining interest and positive standards that critical tasting must be kept alive. It would be a pity to allow our finer perceptions of tasting experience (and resultant range of pleasures) to atrophy. Moreover, I do not think we should feel obliged to re-evaluate, i.e. lower, our standards in the light of technical 'improvements'.

Reasons for tasting

What, then, are the main reasons for tasting? The important thing to realize is that wine will be tasted throughout its life in different places, by different people and for a variety of practical reasons. Here are some of them:

● In the *chai* (*keller, cantina*, whatever local name is given to the producer's cellar), the *maître de chai* or the proprietor will be acting as nurse and midwife. He or she will taste from the moment the grape juice is fermented into wine, watching its condition, balance and development until it is sold or bottled.

● The broker and the merchant prior to making a purchase will also taste from the producer's casks during this period. For the lay amateur, tasting young wine from a barrel in a *chai* – such a romantic-sounding occupation – may be sadly disappointing. Few things can be so starkly raw and scouring as a mouthful of purple new wine. Much better to leave it at this stage to the professionals.

● Samples may have to be submitted by the producer to an official body for a seal of approval. For example, regulations issued in 1974 by the French Government introduced analysis *and tasting* for all *appellation contrôlée* wines.★ The finer German wines are also tasted by a panel before they are awarded a quality seal.

● In the cellars of the local merchant, *négociant* or shipper, the selected wine may be nursed a little further up to the stage of shipment in cask or bottling. During this period, it is tasted by professional buyers with a keen eye on price, style and potential development.

● Competitive tastings at wine fairs and conventions. These are fairly common in wine-producing countries, particularly in California, Australia and eastern Europe.

● After shipment in cask† it will rest in the cellar of the shipper or merchant until it is ready for bottling. The firm's tasters – and the analyst, if there is a laboratory – will examine its condition prior to bottling. Thereafter, from time to time, quality-control personnel will monitor the behaviour and development of the wine in bottle.

● The next category is the trade tasting, where the merchant, wholesaler or restaurateur selects wine for resale. This sort of function may be of the headline-hitting variety in a vast candle-lit cellar, or may take the form of a quiet, down-to-earth event in a rather clinical-looking tasting room. In either case, the buyer is looking for wines either to lay down or to offer for laying down or, of course, for immediate consumption.

● Between trade and consumer come educative tastings and tutorials organized by merchants, wine societies and tasting clubs.

● Lastly, keen amateurs with good cellars will taste their own wines to see how they are progressing and to choose wines suitable for a particular occasion, guest or type of food. They will also taste the wine, before serving, to make sure that its condition and temperature are right.

--------------------- **Tasting contexts** ---------------------

In all the above instances, it will be seen that each taster will be examining a wine in a different context and with a particular point of view: the wine-maker with a parental eye, the buyer with price and market uppermost, the quality-control taster or chemist for condition and stability, the salesman for attractive qualities of price and style, the club member for education and amusement, and the ultimate consumer with palate, pocket and future entertaining plans in mind.

From the second stage to the penultimate, the value of the tasting to the participants will increase roughly proportionately to the range of wines on show. Even at a dinner party, the qualities of a really fine wine will be more fully apparent if paired off with, or preceded by, a lesser but comparable wine.

★The main provisions of Decree 74–871, are as follows:
ARTICLE 1: the wines for which an AOC is claimed cannot be put into circulation without a 'certificate of agreement' issued by the *Institut National des Appellations d'Origine des Vins et Eaux-de-Vie* (INAO) after an examination conforming to the terms of Article II of EEC regulation No. 817/70 of the Council of 28 April 1970.
ARTICLE 2: the examination, organized by INAO or local wine-growing *syndicats*, consists of an analysis and tasting, the latter carried out by a Commission, following officially laid-down procedures.
†To the United Kingdom or elsewhere in Europe. The volume of quality wine being bottled at source is increasing and in many wine areas this is now mandatory. Shipment in cask is not permitted by some countries, notably the U.S.A.

It follows, however, that as each category of taster is apt to be concerned with a limited aspect of wines, their general perspective will narrow, and it is only too easy for the professional and the amateur to adopt, out of habit, a blinkered, one-sided, approach. Professional tasters, with limited time at their disposal and a narrow objective, cannot be expected to probe and analyse the hidden depths of 60 young wines at 10 o'clock in the morning. Nevertheless, they should be conscious of the dangers of slipping into a rut. Equally, amateurs will enrich their experience by taking more than a superficial glimpse at the wonderful liquids that nature, with man's aid, has contrived for their pleasure.

WHEN TO TASTE

The best time for doing anything constructive and creative is when the mental and physical states are freshest. This, for most people (whether they appreciate it or not) is in the morning. It is said, incidentally, that the palate is sharpened by hunger, which would indicate the benefits of preluncheon tasting sessions.

In point of fact, the majority of trade tastings *are* held in the morning. The most quiet and business-like tastings may be held around 10 a.m., possibly at noon. Tastings to which trade or private customers are invited usually begin about 11.30 and may end with a buffet or light luncheon, during the course of which selected wines are shown off against appropriate food. (It is not without significance that the simpler and more wholesome the repast, the better the wines show; there are fewer distractions of flavour. For example, simple cold roast beef and mild English cheeses provide the most perfect foil for good French reds.)

Early evening tastings are also popular. They are generally held by the trade between 6 and 8 p.m. to attract customers who would otherwise find it difficult to attend during their working day. These evening tastings tend to be less serious – people are tired after a day's work and feel more in need of a reviver than the concentration needed to taste in earnest. Or they have had time to go home and change, and may treat the whole affair as a rather jolly social occasion. The wine-merchant host dispensing his or her stock-in-trade may not really mind, so long as the party-goer leaves in a sober enough state to remember the firm's name.

Wine society tastings are also held mainly in the early evenings for similar reasons, though the degree of serious attention is often noticeably higher – perhaps because the members have paid to attend?

General points to observe

Before getting down to the serious business of tasting, there are quite a number of general points to watch out for. Not all are appropriate for professionals and amateurs alike. Some are quite basic, some merely minor details, some may even appear trivial. Not necessarily in order of importance, they are as follows:

No smoking Smoking in a tasting room is not only considered inconsiderate and offensive, it will seriously reduce the effectiveness of other tasters, particularly if they are nonsmokers. It is difficult enough as it is to detect subtleties of bouquet without a nullifying smoke-screen attacking one's nostrils at the same time. For those who doubt this, try puffing smoke into a glass of wine, then sniffing it.

It should be said immediately that the rule of 'no smoking' in the tasting room does not mean that a taster should not smoke at all. There seems little evidence that a smoker's tasting abilities are less than a nonsmoker's. The palate appears to compensate for this regular coating of tobacco smoke and nicotine, and there are numerous examples in the trade of fairly heavy smokers being good tasters. Some are even reputed to have a drag at a strong French cigarette between tasting sessions.

Make notes Remembering the taste of a wine, but forgetting its name, and vice versa, is very tiresome. It is astonishing how easy it is to forget the name of even an outstanding wine only an hour or so after tasting. These blank spots are experienced by the professional, whose memory is cluttered with multitudinous examples, as well as by the novice. It is particularly frustrating for a merchant to recommend a range of wines to a customer and for the latter to say that he or she thought one of them outstanding – only to forget its name.

The answer is, make a note. At least scribble on a piece of paper or in your diary the name of the wine and vintage, and whether it was agreeable or not.

Note making can turn into a fetish; it can become a hobby like collecting stamps. The moderate use of intelligible notes is, however, invaluable, and even a good memory is better served by the briefest record of name, description and opinion. Various methods of note making are dealt with in Chapter VII.

Good company An exchange of views helps to shape and strengthen a hazy impression, revealing aspects of a wine that might not otherwise have been noticed. It goes without saying that the company in question must be equally interested – a large party of casual observers or hard drinkers is merely off-putting.

An organized tasting group is often the best solution, not the least of its virtues being the increased purchasing power of pooled resources which makes it possible to accumulate a wider range of better-class wines.

The main snag about a free-for-all tasting is the distraction of chatterboxes. It is difficult enough as it is without being interrupted between sniffing and note making.

Quite the best advice I can give the newcomer is to taste in the company of an expert, or at least with a taster of some experience.

Related wines It is perfectly possible to judge a fine wine on its own, but its true qualities will be thrown into much sharper perspective when it is tasted alongside another wine, even if dissimilar in style. By far the most revealing type of tasting is one where comparisons can be made between wines of the same vintage but from different districts, or from the same vineyard but of different vintages (*see* p. 62).

Appropriate order of tasting Dry before sweet; young before old; modest before fine. Whether red wines are tasted before white depends on the relative 'weights'. Light dry whites are better before fuller-bodied reds, but light young red wine is better tasted before full-bodied sweet white wine with high extract and residual sugar.

It is perfectly possible for a professional taster to assess the relative qualities of a large range of related wines, say 30 to 60, in a session. It is doubtful, however, whether more than an essential facet or two can be obtained by tasting on this scale, and certainly for beginners, 6 to 10 wines are usually as many as they can effectively cope with. Over this number the taste buds can become tired and the mind confused.

Try to relate the time spent per wine to the total time available and, if necessary, be selective: concentrate on those you particularly wish to taste. Nothing is more frustrating than to find that you have spent nearly all the tasting session on a handful of wines at the lower end of a range, invariably the least interesting, leaving yourself neither time nor energy for the best at the end.

Temperature and presentation Present the wines appropriately: red wines at room temperature, white wines, rosé, champagne, and sherry at cellar temperatures or cooler still (*see* pp. 128–30). Do not draw the corks too far in advance: up to one hour before the tasting is a reasonable average. Decant old and mature wines, as the sediment will swirl up in the bottle after a couple of handlings.

Taste blind 'A sight of the label is worth 50 years' experience' – a cynical truism: for what an impressionable lot we are! Even the most sternly disciplined taster is biased by the merest glimpse of the label, even by the shape of the bottle. One can also be swayed by the appreciative – or otherwise – noises and looks of other tasters.

For a completely objective assessment, arrange the wines to be tasted in numbered glasses (use a wax pencil or stick self-adhesive labels to the upper side of the base), the numbers being related to the bottles which are, of course, out of sight. Alternatively, cover up the bottles, standing the glasses in front. Failing this, turn the bottles round so that the labels cannot be seen.

Don't drink, spit It is nothing short of ridiculous to *drink* one's way through a tasting. How can the last few wines yield more than a hazy impression? This is particularly important when tasting fortified wines.

To taste critically is one thing, to enjoy wines with a meal is another. So when tasting, spit out the wine, don't swallow it. The performance is not considered rude, nor need it be undignified: purse the lips, draw in the cheeks and expel the wine with enough force to project it into the spittoon. It is considered a normal thing to do.

In a *chai* or cellar it is considered perfectly acceptable to spit on the floor, which anyway is often of earth, or, if of concrete, perhaps strewn with sand or sawdust. All proper tasting rooms are furnished with spittoons, often with running water. If a tasting is held in a public building, or in a private room, spittoons must be provided. A wooden wine box containing sawdust is simple to prepare and has the advantage of dimensions generous enough to accommodate all but the very worst shots. It is advisable not to dribble or spit on your host's carpet!

Taste the best Ordinary wines are for drinking, not for philosophical deliberation. Moderate-quality wines afford good practice and can be interesting, but they are often indefinable and rarely clear-cut in character. The most vivid characteristics of a district or a vintage are best exemplified by wines of good quality. In any case, an assessment of lesser wines must inevitably be made in relation to an exemplar or touchstone. Do not be an inverted snob; occasionally buy a great wine and try to see what extra dimensions it has to offer.

Physical hazards Do not waste time trying to taste if you have a streaming cold. Catarrh doesn't help either. Clear your nostrils.

Do not try to taste with traces of alien matter in the mouth. Alkaline toothpaste interacts with the acidity of wine. Fruit, with its high acid content, will affect the taste too; so will highly spiced breakfast sausages. Fish and crabmeat stuck in the teeth are a hazard.

Order and discipline Taste in a regular sequence; examine the appearance of the wine first, its bouquet next and finally its taste. And within those three main subdivisions, look out for definite salient factors. (*See* Chapter V).

A prepared tasting sheet or notebook can be a great help in this respect, and moreover guards against the temptation to leapfrog from wine to wine in a haphazard fashion. This does not mean that one should never dodge back and forth. Indeed, when tasting wines in ascending order of quality or descending order of age, the earlier wines can be seen in sharper perspective if one retastes them after completing the range.

Awareness of context This is highly important and usually underrated. There are several relevant aspects.

The climate as well as the food has to be considered. For example, a charming light wine with a refreshingly high acidity drunk with fresh trout on the banks of the Loire in midsummer, or a vinho verde enjoyed with a rich pork dish in the Minho can taste entirely different on a cold and misty autumn evening with Arbroath smokies in Scotland. Quite apart from the need to match wine with food, the temperature, humidity and time of year have a bearing. The colder the climate, the more full-bodied the wine needs to be, or can be tolerated, and vice versa.

─────────────── **Wine and food** ───────────────

The interrelationship of wine and food is too well known to be restated here. Many books deal with the subject. Suffice it to say that a good wine can be wasted in a wrong food context. It may seem unenterprising, but it is usually safer and more sensible to follow the conventional rules.

What is less well appreciated is that those who are used to tasting mainly fortified wines (sherry; port in particular) may find some difficulty in adjusting their palates to very light table wines. Also, those who are fortunate enough to afford, and to restrict their interest to, only the finest wines will tend to undervalue the quality of much lesser wines. The opposite does not, however, obtain. Regular drinkers of ordinary table wine do not tend to overvalue a fine wine when it is put before them; if anything, they are more likely to be unappreciative of its subtleties and to wonder why anyone would be crazy enough to pay, for one bottle, a sum that might cover their daily fare for a month.

II

ORIGINS OF TASTE CHARACTERISTICS

O for a draught of vintage! that hath been
Cool'd a long age in the deep-delvèd earth.
Keats

I now propose to deal briefly, and necessarily inadequately, for it is a huge subject, with those factors at the growth and production end which create and influence the taste of wine.

It is helpful to have some knowledge of grape varieties, soil, climate, methods of cultivation and wine-making to understand the effects they all have on colour, bouquet and flavour. All this is not, however, necessary for the simple appreciation and enjoyment of wine, so do not please think that you *have* to read about, let alone master, this subject in order to be numbered amongst the world's happy band of wine lovers.

But if you do want to learn more, where do you begin? What has the greatest bearing on the style and flavour of wine? The variety of grape. Is this constant? No, it depends on the soil in which it is grown. Is this combination constant? Again, no; the latitude, climate, the care of the vine and length of fermentation and, of course, the level of human skill at every turn: all these have a bearing.

However, before going into more detail it is important to realize that although it is convenient to break these elements down and study them separately, they can never, in practice, be completely isolated. They interact to create the end product.

———————— GRAPE VARIETIES ————————

Grape varieties are all-important. They have to suit the soil, the climate and the economy of the region. Many good wine books name and describe the main species and varieties, some also deal with vine diseases and pests, grafting and so on; but only a few relate all these to end taste.* What I propose to do here is to list the main varieties in alphabetical order (denoting the most important 'noble' varieties with a star), giving examples of the wine they make. But before I do so, there are a few points worth bearing in mind.

First, it is important to remember that the bulk of the world's wines are of ordinary quality, made from comparatively easy-to-grow, high-yielding vines. Grapes from different varieties may be blended, just as final wines may be. The resulting appearance, smell and taste are usually unremarkable.

Second, the great wines of the world, i.e. those with exceptionally distinctive and refined taste characteristics and quality, are made from a limited range of noble grape varieties, the four leading ones being *cabernet sauvignon*, *riesling*, *pinot* and *chardonnay*. These are produced mainly on difficult, sometimes almost barren, soils and terrains, in delicately uncertain, not to say risky, climates.† Familiarize yourself with these; they give

---

*Outstandingly the best book on the subject is *Vines, Grapes and Wines* by Jancis Robinson (Mitchell Beazley, 1986).

†'Many centuries of experience indicates that only relatively few of the several hundred grape varieties used in making the world's wines are capable of developing the complex aromas and bouquets of the ideal, perfect wine.' Professor A. Dinsmoor Webb, Department of Viticulture and Enology of the University of California, Davis.

the highest satisfaction to the senses, and their characteristics, once mastered, can be more easily memorized than those of lesser varieties. The latter may well be interesting and pleasant, but the fact is that they rarely merit a second glance. Their role is to provide an agreeable accompaniment to a well-cooked meal.

Finally, a highly important factor and one that is often overlooked is the age of the vine. A newly planted vine does not bear wine-making fruit for three years. Thereafter the quality of the fruit increases steadily with age as the roots grow deeper down through soil and subsoil; then for a period the vine combines high quality and substantial yield. Eventually the plant hardens and tires, and its production falls to uneconomic levels.

Aligoté White grape producing minor white wines in Burgundy. Pale; pleasant but undistinguished aroma; dry, light, pleasant acidity.

Alvarinho The principal vinho verde grape, only noticed as a crisp, dry, stylish wine in the better quality brands.

Aramon Prolific 'ordinaire' grown too extensively in the Midi.

Blanc Fumé See *sauvignon blanc*.

Bual White grape making one of the richer madeiras.

Cabernet Franc One of the main Bordeaux varieties. A close relation to the *cabernet sauvignon*, fairly similar in style. Known as *bouchet* in St-Emilion.

*Cabernet Sauvignon Without hesitation, I put *cabernet sauvignon* at the head of the great red-wine grapes of the world, not because I am dogmatic enough to place the finest claret, which it produces, above the finest burgundy, but because it maintains a recognizable style and character even when transplanted out of its classic home region, Bordeaux. For example, a well made 'cabernet' from Australia, California or Chile will have a basic family resemblance despite overtones produced by differences of soils, climate and vinification.

The *cabernet sauvignon* gives red bordeaux (claret) its quality; its depth and richness of colour, aroma and wealth of bouquet; its firm, hard, keeping qualities and length of flavour. The three keys to its recognition are its deep colour, its characteristic aroma of fresh blackcurrants or cedar, and its particular concentrated fruity flavour combined with tannin and acidity. These may all vary in strength and intensity, not only because of differences of soil and microclimate within the Bordeaux area, but because the *cabernet sauvignon* is rarely used alone but grown alongside and combined with other Bordeaux grapes, mainly *cabernet franc* (similar but slightly less distinctive) and *merlot* (softer and plumper).

I think it is useful practice to familiarize yourself with the *cabernet sauvignon* characteristics at their most pronounced. If you are well off, try a good vintage Château Mouton-Rothschild. It has an opacity of colour, opulence of bouquet and concentration of flavour that make it almost a caricature of a great claret. If finances do not run to a first growth try, for grape character, Malescot-Saint-Exupéry or Lynch-Bages of a respectable year. Memorize the grape aroma in particular.

Carignan Prolific and rather neutral red-wine grape (France, North Africa and elsewhere).

*Chardonnay This is the white relation of the *pinot* and makes the great white burgundies of the Côte de Beaune and Chablis (not to forget champagne). It also produces some of the finest varietal wines in California; and it has achieved great success in Australia, New Zealand and even in Italy.

It thrives on chalky soil and produces a wine varying in colour from very pale straw to a fairly pronounced straw-yellow (a feature of many Meursaults and 'New World' wines). A good example will have a fresh, crisp, sometimes smoky, fruity (but not grapey) bouquet – very hard to describe. It will be dry; from the firm steely dryness of chablis, and to some extent of the Puligny-Montrachet, to the softer dryness of Meursault, and the nutty dryness of Corton-Charlemagne. It will have a fair amount of acidity and body, and a subtlety and austerity of flavour that understandably, but paradoxically, attracts claret lovers.

High-quality white burgundies have a rich yet understated flavour; poor ones can be thin and dull. Louis Latour makes a consistently fine Corton-Charlemagne, the Domaine Leflaive good steely Puligny-Montrachet. In California, there are dozens of outstanding wineries; amongst the top: Chateau Montelena, Chalone, Freemark Abbey and the pioneer Stony-hill; and in Australia, Rosemount, Tyrrell, and Petaluma.

Chasselas Another neutral and prolific vine. White.

*Chenin Blanc A major variety making the dry-to-medium-sweet white wines of the mid-Loire. A pleasant waxy aroma, plenty of refreshing acidity. Also grown in California, Australia and South Africa (known as *steen*).

Cinsault Good red grape of the Midi, making the better Tavel and one of the several major permitted varieties used in Châteauneuf-du-Pape.

Fendant The same as *chasselas*. Grown in Switzerland.

Folle Blanche White and ordinary.

Fumé Blanc Californian version of *blanc fumé*; *sauvignon blanc* varietal character.

Fürmint Hungarian white grape producing one of Europe's least-known great classic wines: Tokay. Straw-coloured wines, with a distinctive old-apple-like aroma when young, richly honeyed when aged. Ranging from dry to sweet, finally to concentrated 'essence'.

Gamay This is not a noble grape, but in one region, Beaujolais, it excels and produces a wine of such distinct character that it ranks only just below *pinot* in flavour.

The *gamay* mainly produces a light red wine; often lightish pink-purple in colour and certainly light in alcohol and extract. Its most marked characteristics are a charmingly forthcoming and fruity bouquet, unique in character – difficult to describe but fairly easy to recognize. Lightweight and fresh in the mouth, with little tannin but quite a lot of acidity.

'Grocers' beaujolais' will not do: if you want a fair specimen, choose an unblended single-vineyard wine. Such wines are still not expensive, and most enlightened wine-merchants stock one or two.

*Gewürztraminer In some ways, the most disregarded of the noble grapes. Yet it has an immediately attractive and recognizable style, easy, perhaps too easy, to appreciate and drink, for its opulent flavour tends to overplay its hand and then begins to pall; a white wine, at its best in southern Germany (the Palatinate particularly) and Alsace.

In colour it is sometimes deeper and more yellow than the *riesling*; its most noticeable feature is a scented aroma, reminiscent of lychees, herb-like and spicy (*gewürz*). It ranges from fairly dry to medium-dry; has an equally flowery flavour but is soft and almost velvety, lacking the tinglingly refreshing acidity of the *riesling*.

Of all wine districts, Alsace has the most consistent and reliable producers. It is invidious to recommend just one but for a copybook *gewürztraminer* try one of Trimbach's. The old classic *traminers* of the Palatinate have never been very popular outside Germany and are even losing favour there, being rather earthy, heavyweight, and sometimes clumsy in style. They can, of course, be magnificent. Better to take the advice of a specialist Rhine-wine shipper if you want to taste a good example.

Grenache Fruity, pleasant red wines: lightish in colour but not in alcohol; agreeable, lightly fruity aroma. Grown in the southern Rhône, the Midi, California and Australia.

Gros Plant A synonym for *folle blanche*, making a useful, rather neutral, dry wine in the lower Loire.

Grüner Veltliner Milk-soft, dry white wine from Austria.

Kadarka Red grape grown in Hungary (principal ingredient of Bull's Blood); also in Austria and Yugoslavia.

Malmsey White grape grown in Madeira making a deep amber-brown, sweet dessert wine with characteristic warm, tangy bouquet.

★Merlot A major variety grown in Bordeaux, giving claret flesh and roundness, complementing *cabernet sauvignon*; dominant in Pomerol (Pétrus is a supreme example).

Müller-Thurgau A now well-established *riesling-sylvaner* cross producing a pale-coloured, grapey-scented white wine of easy and attractive character in most German wine districts, particularly in Rheinhessen. Also grown quite successfully in England.

Muscadelle A familiar sounding grape name. One might expect it to be raisiny in smell and flavour, and it is. Usually of very pronounced character, it is used to add particular savour, in sparing quantities, to sweet white bordeaux.

Muscadet Name of grape and type of wine: pale, bone-dry, white, from the lower Loire. Somewhat neutral.

★Muscat Grape producing rich, amber-coloured fortified dessert wine, with tangy aroma, penetrating taste and madeira-like acidity. Grown in several parts of the world but reaching its summit in northeast Victoria (Australia).

Muscat (d'Alsace) This is a somewhat unusual relation of *muscadelle*. It looks like any dry white wine, smells overpoweringly grapey and sweet, but is usually bone-dry on the palate. The best (Hugel produces some fine examples) seem to combine the grapeyness and richness of a *traminer* with the dryness and crispness of a *riesling*.

Nebbiolo One of the great red grapes of Italy, making the deep, powerful, firm and classic Barolo – try one of Marcarini's or Prunotto's – and Barbaresco.

Palomino *The* sherry grape: pale, dry, refined. With *flor* culture develops characteristic zestful bouquet, unmistakable but difficult to describe.

Pedro Ximenez Classic sherry grape used for blending. In Victorian times drunk as a dessert wine: brown, almost opaque; rich, burnt, tangy nose; excessively sweet, rich and heavy.

Petit Verdot Often used as the fourth component, albeit in a small proportion, of red bordeaux. Adds a touch of zest. Slow ripener. A somewhat acidic grape which tends to be green and tart in lesser years.

★Pinot I place the *pinot* second amongst the red grapes of the world, for though (at its best) in Burgundy it produces wines of sublime richness and quality, it does not seem to make wine of so marked and recognizable a character when grown in other districts though wines of pronounced *pinot noir* character are now being made in parts of California and, even more successfully, in Oregon. Perhaps I should mention here that it is also (with its white counterpart) *the* grape of Champagne.

A ripe *pinot*, vinified in a traditional way, from a good *climat* in the Côte de Nuits will have a velvety depth of colour (true burgundy red) with pronounced viscosity ('legs'). However, depth of colour is not a major factor. *Pinot noir* has a thinner skin than *cabernet sauvignon*, hence less pigment and less colour. Its bouquet will be sweeter and more opulent than the *cabernet sauvignon* in Bordeaux; and it will have a consistency on the palate that is both full and soft, alcoholic and velvety. The first main recognition signal is detected by the nose, in particular the *pinot* grape aroma which I, personally, find impossible to describe (though the head of a school of wine once suggested boiled beetroot as a memory trigger). The *pinot* smell must be identified, isolated and memorized. It is only from ripe grapes that the true *pinot* aroma emanates.

The next key factor is the weight of the wine, allied to softness. There is much less of the searingly, mouth-drying tannin of its great rival, the *cabernet sauvignon* – a characteristic which makes a *pinot* much easier to drink even when young.

It is the hardest thing in the world to recommend perfect examples in the modest to middle-priced ranges; perhaps a bit easier in the pricier realms. To discover the flavour and character of a good *pinot* from the Côte de Nuits buy a fine vintage wine bottled by a leading grower such as de Vogüé, Rousseau or Domaine Dujac; or a good Côte de Beaune, from Drouhin; the higher-priced wines of shippers like Jadot or Faiveley; or, if you are rich, La Tâche of a great year.

Pinotage A red grape, a cross between *pinot* and *hermitage*, grown in South Africa, producing a rather jammy, inelegant, alcoholic wine.

Pinot Blanc Once confused with *pinot chardonnay* but, although of similar style, less distinguished.

Pinot Grigio The dry Italian version of *pinot gris*.

Pinot Gris Makes a rather foursquare, somewhat undistinguished, white wine.

*Riesling German wine lovers may place the *riesling* first, but I place it second (to *cabernet sauvignon*) in the hierarchy of noble grape varieties. It is certainly the most versatile and ubiquitous fine white grape, being grown in several European wine districts as well as in almost every major region on other continents. Like the *cabernet sauvignon*, it has consistent strength of character which shows through even after transplanting.

The *riesling* makes a wine with a colour ranging from very pale straw with a hint of green, through pale yellow to deep gold (the latter would be a rich dessert wine, particularly with bottle-age). Its bouquet will be fruity but not grapey, forthcoming, refreshing and clean as a whistle; sometimes flowery, honeyed, and, when made from fully ripe grapes, almost *muscat*-scented. Most *rieslings* are dry to medium-dry, but – another proof of its versatility – it can make the richest and sweetest dessert wines of the world. Another marked feature is a firmness, almost steeliness, of body, and fresh, crisp fruity acidity. In Germany it is never very high in alcohol but has an excellent balance and finish.

The *riesling* scales the greatest heights in the Rheingau, Pfalz and Mosel districts, but can often be seen at its most recognizably straightforward in Alsace.

If I were to suggest a copybook specimen I would choose a *riesling réserve spéciale* or *exceptionnelle* bottled by one of the top Alsatian firms like Hugel. They are remarkably pure wines and very good value.

If you want to take a more opulent hock as an example, I would choose a *reisling spätlese* or *auslese* of the 1989 or 1994 vintages from one of the several distinguished growers such as von Simmern, Dr Weil, von Buhl, Matuschka-Grieffenclau or Bürklin-Wolf.

Rülander Synonym for *pinot gris* making a pleasant, slightly innocuous white wine in the Rhinelands of Germany. Pale coloured, grass-like aroma, mild.

Sangiovese Of the noble grapes of Italy, the principal variety making Chianti. Firm, full, long lasting and with a distinctive dry, almost bitter finish. Try the wines of Antinori or Frescobaldi.

*Sauvignon Blanc A curiously attractive variety; in bouquet and flavour something of a cross between *cabernet sauvignon* and *traminer*. In other words, it combines a spicy, blackcurrant aroma, with a mouth-wateringly refreshing acidity. Fashionable, but can be thin if poor.

It is grown under this name in Bordeaux, and is one of the components of barsac and sauternes, adding the necessary crispness and acidity. Of the same grape family but called *blanc fumé* it is responsible for the wonderfully crisp, dry, fruity wines grown at Pouilly-sur-Loire and for the wines of similar style over the river at Sancerre.

Scheurebe A successful crossing used in Germany, particularly in Rheinhessen and the Palatinate, producing a dramatically grapey aroma and rather facile flavour to match. Lacks the firmness and balance of the *riesling*.

*Sémillon A white grape, one of the major components of sauternes and graves. It has quality and style, a soft lanolin nose, but somehow lacks fruity acidity, which is why it is usually vinified alongside the *sauvignon blanc*.

Sercial Originally the *riesling*, making the palest and driest madeira.

Seyval Blanc A white hybrid quite widely grown in England and making a clean, dry, somewhat neutral, ungrapey but often very satisfactory wine.

Shiraz A red variety extremely at home in Australia and South Africa, making deep-coloured, swiftly maturing yet long-lasting, soft but alcoholic wines reminiscent of the Rhône, with an unmistakable and, at first, strange, tangy aroma aptly described as 'sweaty saddle'.

Siegerrebe Another somewhat exotic, grapey-smelling white variety grown in Germany.

Steen A long-planted variety, similar, probably identical, to the *chenin blanc*. Grown in the Cape vineyards of South Africa and certainly making their best and most characteristic dry white wines.

Sylvaner Though making a familiar Alsatian wine type, *sylvaner* is not a noble grape. It is a more humble but nevertheless distinct variety. It would be both unkind and misleading to describe it as 'the poor man's *riesling*', but it makes a useful dry hock-style wine of less marked character. The *sylvaner* is also grown in Germany, producing a second-rank wine, lacking the finesse and crispness of the *riesling*, except in Franconia where it produces great Steinwein.

Syrah A fine variety grown in the Rhône valley, responsible for red Hermitage: deep, firm long-lasting wines (Paul Jaboulet makes consistently good examples). Also used in Châteauneuf-du-Pape.

Tokay Synonym for the *pinot gris* grown in Alsace. A firm, very satisfactory, dry white wine, yet with few marked characteristics. Not to be confused with Hungarian Tokay.

Traminer See *gewürztraminer*.

Trebbiano A major Italian white-wine grape used in Soave, Orvieto, Chianti and elsewhere, the style depending on the vinification but mainly straw-yellow in colour, with a waxy, rather unfruity, nose; dry, foursquare and rather unexciting flavour and finish.

Viognier An unusual grape which in the Rhône Valley, notably at Condrieu and Château Grillet, makes dry white wine of crispness, style and distinction.

Zinfandel A grape peculiar, and well-suited, to California, making red wines of considerable distinction, many with potential staying power.

SOIL

The taster can comfort himself in the knowledge that convention – historical trial and error – and more recent research work have firmly established exactly what variety of vine flourishes in which type of soil (at any rate in the classic European districts). It is of interest for us to note that the best wines are made from vines grown in uncompromising terrain; often upon ground too poor to support any other crop: schistous rock (port), gravel (claret), slate (mosel), large pebbles (Châteauneuf-du-Pape), and so on.

It seems that soil plays a major but subdued supporting role, at best when unobtrusive, supplying *just* those minerals, storing moisture and so forth, to allow the vine to struggle for existence but no more. Certainly good fertile soil encourages the vine to become overprolific, producing quantity at the expense of quality. Excess use of fertilizers has a similar effect and, in addition, gives undesirable off-tastes to the wine.

Fine white wines, requiring freshness and acidity, thrive on chalk (e.g. fino sherry and champagne). In Burgundy, along the Côte de Beaune, the natural adaptation of vines to soils can be seen dramatically by walking from the red-wine *climats* of Corton round to the chalky slope of Corton-Charlemagne, where only white grapes are grown.

Some wines – red graves, some Rhône and Palatinate wines – smell and taste 'earthy'. Some, as in parts of St-Emilion, reflect the high iron content of the soil by having a taste reminiscent of an iron tonic or one of the more medicinal Australian 'burgundies'. The Napa Valley soil gives its red wines a distinct and recognizable volcanic richness and earthiness.

The importance of the subsoil cannot be overstressed. Much of the richness and extract of a fine wine is drawn from the right sort of subsoil by the deeply thrusting roots of the mature vine.

There are often subtle and complex differences between two red wines made in the same way, from the same grapes, but from neighbouring vineyards. These differences of flavour and bouquet are mainly due to the make-up of soil and subsoil (almost certainly more important) and the balance of minerals. The drainage and the aspect also play a part, mainly in the disposition of moisture and the retention of heat.

Rarely, however, are the effects of soil on taste direct, and when they are these tend to be in the nature of overtones of bouquet and taste, which make their origin the more difficult to pin down. I readily admit to being ill-equipped to delve deeply into the fascinating substrata of soil and mineral tastes. At least the taster should be aware of their presence and indubitable influence, and should try to recognize those soil characteristics that are pronounced.

CLIMATE

After the indefinable complexities of soils, the effects of climatic variations are more frequently documented and more easily understood. Like soil, climate influences the taste of wine through its effect on the grape. Understand the reaction of the grape to sun, cold and rain, and it is easier to recognize the end product of a given vintage.

Geographical influences – the limits of latitude, proximity of rivers and bodies of water and height above sea level – can take a back seat, from the taster's point of view. The wines we normally come across will not be grown in unsuitable areas. This is not our problem. Climatic variations, however, are of considerable interest and significance.

There are three broad aspects of climate in so far as they affect wine:

Zones The first concerns the consideration and comparison of the effects of two quite different climes: the gentle but significant variations in a temperate zone, the northern half of Europe, for example, and the less variable, hotter and drier zones exemplified by North Africa, the uplands of South Africa, the irrigated areas of South Australia and southern California.★ The comparative uniformity and reliability of the warmer areas make life less hazardous for the grower but somewhat less interesting for the discerning drinker, as the wine is of a more even quality, with fewer surprises, and rarely, if ever, scales the heights. The motto of fine wine could well be *nil sine labore*, for it is the struggle against the elements that kindles quality.

Annual differences The second aspect of climate is confined to the temperate zones. It consists of the annual variation and is of enormous importance to the entire concept of vintage wines. This aspect will be dealt with in some detail below.

Microclimate The third aspect is the microclimate: the variations due to the lie of the land – sun traps, the susceptibility to pockets of frost and fog, etc., which occur within wine areas and from vineyard to vineyard.

The connoisseur will mainly be concerned with the second aspect, vintage variations, but in the process of describing the general effects of too much sun and too much rain, the implications will throw light on the extremes of the first aspect: that is to say, the character of wines made at the edges of the permissible vine-growing latitudes will reflect the characteristics outlined below.

Variations Too much sun and too little rain (in a given year or in a particular part of the world) will reduce the quantity of juice in the grape, thicken the skins and maximize the sugar content, thus producing excess colouring matter, tannin and alcohol. In some northern zones, at the end of the ripening

★California has been scientifically divided into five climatic regions based on average sun/heat levels.

period the skins may shrivel and crack, letting in undesirable ferments. The first fermentation may be hard to control, risking spoilage. (Choice of grape, soil, irrigation and vat cooling systems are counter factors in hot, dry areas.) As a result, the wines, if red, will be full of colour, alcohol and tannin, heavy, coarse and hard. If white they will lack acidity and, in consequence, be heavy, flat, flabby, charmless, and with little bouquet.

Too much rain and insufficient sun will increase the volume of juice. However, the grapes will not ripen fully, so the sugar content will be low, and the wrong sort of acidity high. This will result in a low alcoholic content and pale colour (if red). The wine will be thin and tart, unbalanced and short-lived. If steps are taken during vinification to increase the sugar content artificially, and to stabilize the wine, it can be made into a tolerable beverage but will never be fine.

Vintage Charts

Those much maligned aids, vintage charts, do at least provide a handy *aide-mémoire*, for their ratings, in effect, summarize the overall weather conditions which have affected a particular area in a given year. For example, the year 1977 rates 2 out of 7 under the 'Red Bordeaux' heading of the current Wine & Food Society Vintage Chart. This low rating reflects the poor weather prevailing that year in Bordeaux, resulting in equally poor wine. However, the north of Portugal enjoyed an excellent combination of sun and rainfall in 1977. Under the heading 'Port' it justly rates 7 out of 7.★

It is with vintages like 1964 that generalizations become dangerous. Heavy rainstorms in the middle of the vintage were disastrous for those Bordeaux growers who were holding on for further ripening. The early, pre-rain pickers like Château Latour were fortunate. The late pickers, including Lafite, Mouton-Rothschild, Calon-Ségur and Lynch-Bages, made comparatively puny, wishy-washy wines. Over the river, in St-Emilion, the rain was not as severe as in the Médoc and the wines were uniformly more successful. Charts *can* be useful, but watch out for the exceptions. But, better a generalization than no information at all.

My tip for beginners is not to be bamboozled and bedazzled by airy-fairy vintage talk. Forget the bottle and label for a minute and remember the precious liquid inside stems from a crop affected by weather conditions like other crops. It would all come more naturally, for the English at any rate, if we were to realize that on the rare occasions when we have enjoyed a really hot summer the odds are that the rest of northern Europe has too, and that the vintage will probably be particularly good, and vice versa.

WINE-MAKING

Whereas the care of the vine – the annual toil in the vineyards – can vary in degree and attention from grower to grower, we can reasonably assume a tolerable standard, to enable them to earn a living. Their husbandry will affect quality and quantity; the overuse of certain fertilizers may also affect the taste, but it is

★This important subject is exhaustively covered in *The Great Vintage Wine Book II* by Michael Broadbent (Mitchell Beazley, 1991) and succinctly summarised in Michael Broadbent's Pocket Guide to Wine Vintages (Mitchell Beazley 1995).

when we come to wine-making that the skills and particular techniques of the owner, manager or cellar-master will have the most direct bearing on the colour, bouquet and flavour of the wine produced.

―――――――――― **Improvements** ――――――――――

Thanks to the activity of schools of oenology and viticulture, to governmental and local institutes and advisory bodies, much less bad wine is made these days. It is, however, totally untrue for them to claim that without their help and advice no good wine would be made. Great wines were made before oenology, as an exact science, was conceived; just as wine was sold before marketing concepts were devised. The sciences and pseudosciences are servants and modern aids; rarely the originators, never the masters.

In the more ignorant and uncontrolled days of the past, galloping fermentation by wild yeasts would frequently give an off-taste to the wine, overhot fermentation might breed microbes in the absence of sulphur dioxide and the heat would usually 'cook' the wines; sulphur would be overused, and so on. All these errors and omissions could spoil the smell and taste in some detectable way. Nowadays, so far as red wines are concerned, the principal worry is that the demands of commerce – wines for quick maturing and quick turnover – are being met by speedier fermentation and increased blending. The former leads to paler coloured red wines with less tannin and extract, the latter to neutralization of character and quality.

―――――――――――― **Care** ――――――――――――

Care of the wine prior to bottling – or the lack of it – can have a direct effect on taste. For example, the sharp spiciness which comes from wines being kept too long in new casks, or musty woodiness from too long in old; the acrid effect of over-sulphuring; the sour overtones of a wine left on the lees too long, and the vinegary smell of a pricked, probably neglected, wine.

―――――――――― **THE EFFECT OF AGE** ――――――――――

It is a useful oversimplification to say that wine is a living thing. It implies, quite correctly, that wine, once made, is in a constant state of change and development, first in cask, then in bottle. Again, for simplicity, I am ignoring the use and effects of glass-lined vats, ionization, pasteurization, refrigeration and all the sophisticated tools and techniques employed these days by large undertakings to keep their wines as stable as possible. My terms of reference here are limited to the ageing of *quality* vintage wines, in so far as they affect taste.

―――――――――― **Quality and maturity** ――――――――――

Perhaps I should define 'quality vintage wine' or *vin de garde*. It is a wine made from the grapes grown in one good vineyard★ of one vintage whose raw young components are present in strength and balance, needing a period of years, first in cask, but mainly in bottle, to marry, settle and soften into one harmonious but characterful whole.

Red wines Young red wine will start life with a full colour,

★The grapes from which a particular *marque* of vintage port or champagne is made might come from one or more vineyards, but will be under the control of a single firm.

tannins, acidity and alcohol. Over a period of time, depending on the strength and degree of these basic elements, the colouring matter will be precipitated by the tannins (*see* p. 50), which themselves gradually lose their harsh dryness. The acidity will tone down, and the whole ensemble will look more mellow, smell sweeter and richer, with subtler overtones and scents, and the effect in the mouth will also be soft, mellow and harmonious – no discordant edges – with layers of flavour and a long finish and fragrant aftertaste.

Red wines repay keeping best. But do *all* red wines repay keeping? The answer is no. Cheap branded wines, nonvintage blended wines are not meant to be kept. Very minor clarets and burgundies will probably improve with a few months' to a couple of years' bottle-age in your cellar (do not rely on the merchant to give an ordinary wine bottle-age, he will endeavour to sell it soon after bottling). Even well-made but minor *bourgeois* wines, claret in particular, are not worth holding overlong. It is important to keep things in perspective and realize that a 20-year-old *bourgeois* claret will not have improved to classed-growth quality simply by keeping. It may have softened and mellowed a little, but in the final analysis it will only taste like a minor claret, not finer but older, more tired and possibly sadder!

White wines It is commonly accepted that *dry* white wines are not meant to be kept, but to be drunk whilst young and fresh. What is little known is that the really good dry whites, particularly from classic districts, not only keep well but will develop with bottle-age quite distinctive qualities of colour, bouquet and flavour. For example, a 1966 Montrachet, a 1952 Corton-Charlemagne, a 1947 Vouvray, many 1959 Rhine wines of quality, from a good cold cellar, can still be on the plateau of perfection now, in the mid 1990s. In financial terms, unlike their red equivalents, they may not have appreciated proportionately in value; but in sensory terms they can be a revelation. Which really is what tasting is all about. . . .

Elders and betters? Summing up, don't expect age to confer upon an ordinary or middle-class wine qualities it never had to begin with. The only wines that will keep and blossom in interest and character over the years are the pedigree wines: first-growth claret and some of the other classified growths; single-vineyard burgundies bottled at the domaine; the rare aristocratic Chiantis and Barolos; great dessert wines like vintage port, Tokay *aszu*, sauternes, sweet Loire wines (particularly Coteaux du Layon) and Rhine and Mosel wines of *Auslese*, *Beerenauslese* and *Trockenbeerenauslese* quality; and also the top-quality premium wines of Australia and California.

III

MAIN REGIONAL CHARACTERISTICS

*Planting a vineyard and making wine
is a gentleman's occupation,
and the highest type of agriculture.*
Frona Eunice Wait
Wines and Vines of California, 1889

This chapter is an attempt to give the reader some indication of what to expect when faced with a wine from a major region or district or type.

Rather than give a blow-by-blow description of each wine, which would require a gazeteer not a chapter, I will endeavour to point out those salient features which are most characteristic, most distinctive or unusual. It might be helpful to keep a marker in the 'Grape variety' section of Chapter II, and another in the glossary in Chapter XII.

The following arrangement is by country, district and type. Good, bad and indifferent vintages are listed, and finally, in chart form, there is a breakdown of wines into dry, sweet, light and heavy. If the structure is rather rigid and the generalizations too broad, I nevertheless feel that some guidance is better than no guidance at all. As tasting is so subjective, it is up to you, the reader, to develop your own pattern of knowledge and to clothe it with your own tasting experiences.

FRANCE

Red, white, dry, sweet, sparkling, fortified with brandy, *liquoreux*, spice-augmented, common-or-garden to finest and rarest: France produces the whole gamut. Here is a brief description of the major districts and the types of wine produced.

BORDEAUX (RED)

Claret is thought of as a light table wine. It can, however, vary from deep-coloured and heavy to 'clairet', palish and light, depending on district, vintage weather, vineyard site and vinification.

─────────── *Médoc* ───────────

The classic claret area: firm dry wines, purple and tannic when young, elegant and harmonious when mature. Life span depends on vintage, weight and class of wine. These are the main districts:

Pauillac Depth and concentration of colour, opaque and purple when young; pronounced and concentrated *cabernet sauvignon* aroma and flavour (*see* p. 14), marked tannin and acidity when immature. The greatest wines for keeping and development. Home of three first-growths: Lafite, Latour and Mouton-Rothschild.

St-Estèphe Deep colour; stark, raw, fruity nose, *cabernet* less marked; full, firm, tannic. Slow-developing, solid wines, from heavier clay soil.

St-Julien Copybook claret. Lighter; more cedary bouquet;

balance, elegance, harmony. Not the longest-living but capable of great finesse.

Margaux Quite variable in style but on the whole similar in colour and weight to St-Julien; bouquet complex and fragrant. Develops well.

Moulis, Listrac, Soussans and St-Laurent These middle-Médoc and hinterland districts, noted mainly for good *bourgeois* growths, produce fruity and dry wines but without the strongly marked characteristics of greater districts and vineyards. Will keep, but generally not worth keeping too long.

Graves

Similar weight to Médoc but develops more quickly. Garnet-coloured, showing red-brown tinge sooner. Bouquet and flavour notably earthy, both being loose-knit, soft and rounded.

Pomerol

Two styles: one deep and firm but with full, fleshy *merlot* richness, slow developing; the other lighter in colour and weight, sweeter, more gentle and quick-maturing. Each style has a noticeably velvety texture in the mouth. Lighter vintages develop quickly.

St-Emilion

Two styles: from the 'Côtes' around the town, deepish but quick-maturing wines, loose-knit, sweeter on bouquet and palate; easy, flavoury. From the 'Graves' plateau next to Pomerol, firm, fine fruity wines, with depth of colour and flavour, with hint of iron/earth character detectable on nose and palate.

Fronsac

Good deep-coloured wines; hard, fruity bouquet and flavour, tannic and needing bottle-age though rarely capable of great development. Like a firm, hard Pomerol. Austere but pure and characterful.

Bourg and Blaye

The poor man's Médoc – if I may so categorize without wishing to give offence. Dry, straightforward, rather coarse wines: plain but honest. Need a little bottle-age but not worth cellaring for 10 years – all you will have is a still somewhat coarse minor wine, 10 years older.

Claret vintages

Great: 1928, 1929, 1945, 1947, 1949, 1953, 1959, 1961, 1982, 1989, 1990. *Very good:* 1934, 1955, 1962, 1964, 1966, 1970, 1971, 1985, 1986, 1988. *Quite good:* 1943, 1952, 1975, 1976, 1978, 1979, 1981, 1983, 1994. *Variable:* 1948, 1950, 1954, 1957, 1958, 1960, 1967, 1969, 1973, 1980, 1984, 1987, 1991, 1993. *Poor:* 1951, 1956, 1963, 1965, 1968, 1972, 1974, 1977, 1992.

Maturity span

Great wines: 12 to 30 years; *good wines:* 8 to 20; *lesser wines:* 5 to 10.

BORDEAUX (WHITE)

Two ranges: from very dry to medium-dry, and from medium-sweet to very sweet; colour from very pale yellow-straw (more yellow in a hot vintage), golden-tinged with bottle-age, to the deep old-gold of venerable sauternes. Note the soft lanolin fragrance of the *sémillon* grape, the fresh and mouth-watering *sauvignon blanc*, which in combination are deep, rich and honeyed when fully mature.

Graves

Colour range: pale to straw-yellow. Very dry to medium-dry, with more body and less of the mouth-puckering acidity of Loire whites, less fruity-fragrant than hock. At best, refined; improves with 5 to 10 years' bottle-age. The less-than-best can be thin, short, dull, stodgy, uninspiring. All except the few top growths should be drunk young.

Sauternes

Deep, more golden in colour. Characteristic honeyed overripe grape smell from *pourriture noble*. Essentially sweet, luscious and full-bodied though varying in weight and richness, depending on the year, and neatly counter-balanced by acidity. Note particularly the concentration and aftertaste of the really great wines. Fine sauternes not only keep well, they really need bottle-age.

Barsac Similar in style and content though sometimes paler, green-tinged when young; often more refreshingly forthcoming bouquet; slightly lighter in body and less rich, particularly in minor vintages.

Sauternes vintages

Great: 1945, 1947, 1949, 1955, 1959, 1967, 1975, 1983, 1988, 1989, 1990. *Very good:* 1953, 1962, 1971, 1976, 1986. *Good:* 1952, 1957, 1961, 1966, 1970, 1979, 1982, 1985. *Variable:* 1948, 1950, 1958, 1969, 1972, 1973, 1978, 1980, 1981, 1984, 1991, 1994. *Poor:* 1946, 1951, 1954, 1956, 1960, 1963–65, 1968, 1974, 1977, 1987, 1992, 1993.

Maturity span

Great sauternes: 10 to 100 years; at peak 20 to 30. *Good sauternes:* 8 to 40; at peak 10 to 20. *Lesser wines:* 3 to 10; peak 4 to 8. *Finest graves*, dry white bordeaux of very good vintages have a 10 to 30 year life span.

BURGUNDY (RED)

It is difficult to generalize about burgundies. Often the dominant factor is a grower's or merchant's style. Nevertheless, burgundy is essentially different in character, weight and development to claret, and subject to great variations of colour and body (and quality). At best, deep, rich colour; fine ripe *pinot* aroma and fragrance; fairly alcoholic yet velvety, and quicker developing thanks to less tannic astringency, the result of the *pinot* grape variety, climate and vinification methods.

Côte de Nuits

The main classic red burgundy area capable of producing full, firm long-lasting wines. By commune or village-district:

Gevrey-Chambertin At its best – good vintage, great vineyard, top grower – deep-coloured, inimitable bouquet: rich, masculine, complex, with meaty *pinot* aroma; full-bodied, firm yet velvety and long-lasting.

Chambolle-Musigny Almost the opposite: lighter, more gentle, feminine, elegant; noted for fragrance of bouquet. The 'Margaux' of the Côte de Nuits.

Morey-St-Denis Two styles: one big and fruity, the other lighter and looser-textured. At best firm and elegant. Sometimes 'fluffy' and short-lived.

Vougeot The famous Clos is much subdivided, and variable. Hope for a fairly full, firm, flavoury, long-lasting wine.

Echézeaux Just above Vougeot, more close-knit and elegant; refined, some delicacy.

Vosne-Romanée The centre, the heart of the Côte de Nuits. Colour variable in depth; bouquet rich, fragrant and capable of extraordinary opulence, even spicy. On the palate, deep, rich, velvety but not heavy. At best the epitome of burgundian elegance and style.

Nuits-St-Georges At best 'copybook', but without the majesty of Chambertin or regal opulence of Vosne-Romanée. Agreeable, fullish, firm, flavoury. Note the smoky oak-reminiscent *pinot* aroma and flavour of some of the finer domaines such as Henri Gouges.

Côte de Beaune

Generally more loose-grained, less concentrated and shorter life span than Nuits. Easy and agreeable, but as with all burgundy, only the best domaines will give a true picture of the *pinot* grape and district styles.

Aloxe-Corton No more than pleasant, medium-weight wines except for Le Corton and the top vineyards which sometimes match Chambertin in weight, with full, meaty, slightly roasted *pinot* aroma and flavour. Long-lasting.

Beaune The centre, geographically and in style. At best, not too full, elegant, good *pinot* flavour and balance.

Pommard Not dissimilar, but in Epenots and Rugiens produces very distinguished, fruity wines which develop and keep well.

Volnay Lighter in colour and style; firm, elegant, a certain delicacy. Equivalent to Chambolle-Musigny in the Côte de Nuits, but lower keyed.

Santenay The most southerly of the Côtes, and relatively minor. True Santenay is light in colour and frankly no more than pleasant. Do not expect great depth or finesse.

Red burgundy vintages

Great: 1945, 1949, 1959, 1971, 1978, 1985, 1988, 1990. *Very good:* 1947, 1952, 1953, 1962, 1964, 1966, 1969, 1976, 1983, 1986, 1989. *Good:* 1955, 1961, 1970, 1979, 1987, 1992, 1993. *Quite good:* 1948, 1954, 1957, 1958, 1967, 1972, 1980, 1981, 1982, 1994. *Variable:* 1950, 1963, 1973, 1984, 1991. *Poor:* 1946, 1951, 1956, 1960, 1965, 1968, 1974, 1975, 1977.

Maturity span

Great wines: 8 to 30 years. *Good wines:* 6 to 15. *Lesser wines:* 3 to 8. (Some top-class wines of the 1920s are still most attractive. It is hard to generalize.)

BURGUNDY (WHITE)

Virtually all white burgundy is pale in colour, and dry. Exceptionally hot vintage years will produce a deeper colour, more body and very slight sweetness, and wine from top-class vineyards in other fine years may also have more colour and richness.

Chablis

Noted for its appealing pale straw-yellow colour with greenish tinge; for its firm, steely bouquet; and in particular, for its dryness and crisp, rapier-like quality: austere yet subtle and long-flavoured.

Côte de Beaune

Puligny-Montrachet In weight and style not unlike chablis but the best have a noticeable and very fragrant smoky *chardonnay* aroma. Firm, crisp, refreshing on the palate. 'Copybook' white burgundy. Leflaive is supreme.

Le Montrachet Rich, yellow colour, shot with gold as it matures; deep, complex, rich, smoky bouquet. Dry, warm, nutty, long flavour, fragrant aftertaste. Small production. Expensive.

Bâtard-Montrachet Fine, full, dry, oaky. Substantial and of high quality.

Chevalier-Montrachet Refined, lighter, elegant.

Chassagne-Montrachet Not unlike its neighbouring commune, Puligny, but perhaps slightly less elegant, less austere. (Also produces excellent red wine.)

Meursault Often yellower in colour; fine bouquet; broader texture and character.

Corton-Charlemagne Noted for its full, nutty, vanilla-oak aroma and flavour. Full-bodied, long-lasting.

White burgundy vintages

Very good: 1961, 1962, 1966, 1967, 1969, 1971, 1973, 1976, 1978, 1979, 1983, 1986, 1989, 1990. *Good:* 1964, 1970, 1982, 1985, 1987, 1988, 1992, 1994. *Quite good/variable:* 1963, 1972, 1974, 1977, 1980, 1981, 1984, 1991, 1993. *Poor:* 1965, 1968, 1975.

SOUTH BURGUNDY

South of the Côte d'Or, between Chagny and the outskirts of Lyon, are a string of relatively minor districts producing pleasing, fairly distinctive but not particularly distinguished wines.

Chalonnais

Rully and Mercurey make stylish, medium-light red wines of a generally burgundian character; fruity, and best drunk fairly young. Montagny makes good, well-balanced, dry white wine, pleasing but not great.

Mâconnais

Mâcon rouge and Mâcon blanc are at best agreeable, clean, wholesome lightish red and dry white. Do not expect more. Pouilly-Fuissé, though a cut above, is overrated and overpriced. At best it is pale, dry, clean and crisp; no great subtlety or memorable distinction.

Beaujolais

There are two sorts of genuine beaujolais: the currently fashionable, modern-vinified wines which take a lead from beaujolais nouveau. Their characteristics are a palish, pink-red colour; very pronounced, almost scented *gamay* aroma; dry, very light (thin in poorer years), flavoury, and with marked, refreshing acidity. To be drunk young. However, the finest, worth seeking out, are still the unblended single-vineyard wines made by older methods: deeper and more substantial in colour and body, with a deep, elegant, more vinous *gamay* bouquet and flavour, which improves with some bottle-age. (Not to be confused with the plummy, stewed, characterless, commercial 'grocer's' beaujolais.)

Beaujolais blanc is pale and dry, often with slightly more body than Mâcon blanc or even Pouilly-Fuissé.

Beaujolais vintages

The rare classic years: 1967, 1969, 1970, 1971, 1973, 1976, 1983, 1985, 1989, 1990. Avoid poor years. Though made every year it is not consistent. Beaujolais can be thin, feeble and bitter. Much is undistinguished and overpriced.

RHÔNE (RED)

The main characteristics of the Rhône reflect the nature of the terrain, and sun. Deep and very purple when young; full, heavy, alcoholic, less elegant, less acidity than burgundy. Bouquet the least interesting feature.

Châteauneuf-du-Pape

Most people's idea of a Rhône wine: deep-coloured (unless a poor year or speedy vinification), foursquare, hefty, fruity, soft yet good balance. Bouquet vinous, but no strong varietal aroma owing to the *mélange* of grapes. Tannin and acidity less marked than in bordeaux.

Hermitage

Although deep and purple when young, a contrast to Châteauneuf in style: less heavy, with finer bouquet, considerable fruit, more refinement and balance. Sometimes claret-like. Improves with maturity.

Côte Rôtie

Some of the weight and heat of Châteauneuf, with the style and elegance of Hermitage. Fine, long-lasting.

Lirac, Ventoux, Gigondas

Although from the hot southern Rhône, making lighter, almost beaujolais-like wines, at best delightful, fruity and not too serious; often lacking depth and finesse.

Tavel rosé

The nearest rosé to a red wine. Tavel's most notable feature is its dryness, body and certain austerity. Less frivolous than most rosés.

RHÔNE (WHITE)

Palish in colour, more body than white burgundies, and less acidity. Bouquet not very marked save for really good Hermitage blanc, Condrieu and Château Grillet.

Châteauneuf-du-Pape blanc

Not often seen, but in a good year slightly sweet and with unusual character. Fullish colour and body; deep, rich.

Hermitage blanc

A lemon-tinged straw colour; a squeeze of lemon peel in the often stylish bouquet and flavour. Dry, often refined.

Condrieu

Fine and rare, dry and nutty, complex with great length.

─────────────── **Château Grillet** ───────────────

Unusual, and deserving its unique appellation. In a good year (e.g. 1989) deep yellow in colour; vinous, rich, slightly smoky bouquet; dryish, fairly full, rich, stylish, original, slightly caramel-tinged flavour.

─────────────── **Rhône vintages** ───────────────

Great: 1945, 1949, 1952, 1959, 1961, 1971, 1978, 1983, 1985, 1990. *Very good:* 1947, 1953, 1955, 1957, 1962, 1964, 1966, 1967, 1970, 1979, 1982, 1988, 1989. *Good:* 1969, 1972, 1980, 1986, 1991, 1992. *Variable:* 1960, 1973, 1974, 1976, 1977, 1981, 1984, 1987, 1993, 1994. *Poor:* 1956, 1958, 1963, 1965, 1968, 1975.

LOIRE

Total contrast to Rhône. Mainly white, very dry to medium-dry; lighter, with pronounced refreshing acidity.

Sancerre and Pouilly-Fumé Both pale, slightly green-tinged; forthcoming, piquant, raw blackcurrant *sauvignon blanc* aroma; very dry, light (thin in poor years), a piquant fruitiness and high acidity. Overfashionable.

Vouvray Although with high acidity, much broader in style than Sancerre, with pleasant, not very pronounced, waxy-vanilla aroma. Both dry and medium-sweet (*demi-sec*). The latter can be long-lasting, developing honeyed richness. Also pleasing *pétillant* and sparkling wines.

Saumur Thin but flavoury whites and red (Champigny). Excellent sparkling wines, lively with attractive grapey aroma, medium-dry, light and clean.

Chinon and Bourgueil The two main red-wine districts. Medium, beaujolais-like colour: violet when young. Marked piquant raspberry-like aroma. Dry, light, very flavoury and fruity, but tart and thin in lesser years.

Savennières Yellow; elegant waxy bouquet; dry, firm, elegant and finely balanced.

Coteaux du Layon Yellow; rather underplayed lanolin aroma that deepens and improves with age. Main features: semi-sweetness, rich, ripe, attractive fruitiness and marked acidity. Bonnezeaux and Quarts-de-Chaume keep magnificently, indeed need bottle-age. Good summer-pudding wines.

Muscadet Near to nondescript in colour and bouquet; pretty low-keyed in flavour too. Main feature bone-dryness, but clean, zestful, the best refined.

─────────────── **Loire vintages** ───────────────

Great: 1947, 1949, 1959, 1964, 1989, 1990. *Very good:* 1945, 1962, 1976, 1985, 1986, 1988. *Good:* 1953, 1961, 1966, 1969, 1971, 1975, 1978, 1979, 1982. *Variable:* 1955, 1970, 1973, 1974, 1980, 1981, 1983, 1984, 1987, 1991, 1992, 1993, 1994.

ALSACE

In Alsace, the wines are named after grape variety not district. Virtually all are white, most are dry; overall honest and reliable.

Riesling Main features: fragrance; firm fruit and steeliness of flavour; dry, crisp acidity.

Gewurztraminer Main features: spicy-grapey bouquet and flavour. Soft, fatter, less acid.

Muscat Assertive grapey bouquet, but surprisingly dry, sometimes austere.

Tokay, Pinot Gris Less distinctive but good dry wines, perhaps overshadowed by the first two classic grapes.

Sylvaner Less pronounced characteristics. Dry, mild.

─────────────── **Alsace vintages** ───────────────
Great: 1959, 1961, 1971, 1976, 1983, 1989, 1990. *Very good:* 1964, 1981, 1985, 1988, 1992, 1993. *Good:* 1966, 1967, 1973, 1975, 1986, 1991. *Good enough:* 1969, 1970, 1978, 1979, 1982, 1987, 1994.

CHAMPAGNE

All-important is the name of the *marque*, though most major champagne houses produce a de luxe blend of some refinement and distinction. Whether the full, meaty classics (like Krug and Bollinger) or pale, light *blanc de blancs* (Taittinger for example), the essential characteristics of a fine champagne are:

Appearance: appealing palish colour with a steady, continuous flow of small, evenly spaced bubbles. With age the colour deepens to gold, sparkle less lively.

Bouquet: firm, creamy, vinous, with either a rich meaty style or a nutty, smoky-charred *pinot chardonnay* aroma.

Palate: bone-dry to dryish; light and firm to full, depending on the house style. What distinguishes fine champagne from other sparkling wines is finesse, elegance, length of flavour and crisp, positive finish.

─────────────── **Champagne vintages** ───────────────
Great: 1945, 1952, 1964, 1971, 1985. *Very good:* 1947, 1949, 1953, 1955, 1959, 1961, 1962, 1966, 1970, 1976, 1979, 1982, 1992. *Good:* 1969, 1973, 1975, 1978, 1980, 1981, 1983.
1991, 1993 and 1994 will not be 'vintage' years.

CAHORS

Although recently upgraded, the wines from this famous old area are rarely seen outside France, and the 'black' Cahors almost never. At best deep characterful substantial reds, soft, fullish, long-lasting.

MIDI

The Gard, Hérault and Aude areas produce a vast amount of white and red – but little for the connoisseur to linger over. At best they make agreeable table wines. Some, like Fitou, have character and flavour. Some new, small vineyards now produce remarkable quality, in particular St-Jean de Bébian and Mas de Daumas Gassac. Classic, but little seen outside France, are the *vins doux naturels*: muted sweet dessert wines such as Lunel, Muscat de Frontignan and (in the Rhône) Beaumes de Venise – palish tawny in colour, attractive, muscat grapey aroma, sweet and fullish but not heavy like port; easy, raisiny-flavoured wines with refreshing end-acidity.

PROVENCE

Solid, respectable but stodgy reds; dry, rather unexciting whites; and dry, rather zestless rosés, the main attraction being a fancy bottle. Fine for drinking on the spot. Affords the peripatetic wine lover happy explorations to discover the occasional outstanding domaine, such as Ott (their rosé best served at room temperature) and Vignelaure (deep, distinguished, tannic red). Bandol can be good.

JURA

Frankly, the red, white, rosé and sparkling wines from this area, with a few exceptions, are sound, quite appealing but commercial, bland and fairly undistinguished. The Jura is, however, the cradle of one of the most original wines in the world: the *vin jaune* of Château-Chalon. Yellow in colour, with strange, nutty bouquet; dry, austere, fairly full-bodied: a cross between an old fino sherry and Tokay *szamorodni*.

The white wine of Etoile is very dry, straw-flavoured and of good quality. Nearby, Château d'Arlay makes dry white wine of rare distinction.

GERMANY

From the point of view of the connoisseur, German wines are white, ranging from dry and light to exceptionally sweet and rich; in quality and style between insubstantial and short, to deep, rich, refined and long-flavoured. There is much bland commercial 'sugar and water' wine.

The range, thanks to oenology and the 1971 German wine laws, is infintely less varied than of old. Real character and quality depend on dedicated growers. Happily, there are still quite a few left.

The essential thing to bear in mind is that the German wine-makers' ideal is 'fruity-acidity': a combination of delicacy, ripe-grapey quality, fragrance and refreshing acidity. However, owing to advanced wine-making techniques and a rather contrived efficiency, quality standards are levelling out and the grape style, sweetness and consistency seem to mask district, soil, microclimate and other local variations. Perhaps the ideal is now too easily reached at the expense of character and individuality. Nevertheless, the great estates in the classic areas continue to produce fine wines. Quality and vintage variations are still very important.

The drinkers of German wines should confine themselves to the clearly defined fine wines *(Qualitätswein mit Prädikat)*:

● *Kabinett:* natural, unsugared wines of some quality.

● *Spätlese:* late-picked, i.e. ripe grapes. Intensity, weight, character and sweetness vary from district to district, grower to grower, year to year, but generally speaking, palish in colour, dry to medium-dry.

● *Auslese:* from selected riper bunches. As with *Spätlesen*, variations of sweetness and body depend on place and vintage. *Auslese* wine is richer, riper, usually, but not necessarily, sweeter, and of fine quality.

● *Beerenauslese:* from individually selected very ripe grapes. Usually a deeper yellow-gold in colour; most characteristic bouquet: rich, ripe, honeyed scent of *Edelfäule*. On the palate: sweet, fullish, rich, ripe, often grapey, with fine balancing acidity. Becomes softer and more complex with age. Long lasting.

● *Trockenbeerenauslese:* only in certain years, from select, overripe, shrivelled grapes. Yellow-gold, deepening to fine old-gold with age; concentrated essence-of-grapes aroma, often raisiny but when immature less assertive than the smell of *Beerenauslesen*. Very sweet, very rich, highly concentrated; often with low alcohol but high degrees of sugar and acidity. The world's rarest and richest dessert wines. Very long lasting.

RHEINGAU

Riesling reigns supreme in this district and produces fine, firm, steely wines with intense bouquet and· fragrance; dry to medium-dry, long finish. Also, in suitably fine years, outstanding dessert wines with incredible concentration, richness and refinement. Long lasting. Districts provide thematic variations: for example, Eltville wines are light but firm and elegant, Rauenthal rich, almost spicy, Hochheim masculine, foursquare, more earthy.

RHEINHESSEN

Generally softer, more open, less condensed, attractive, ripe fruity wines.

PFALZ (PALATINATE)

Germany's most southerly great wine district, just north of Alsace. Essentially more substantial, deep, grapey wines. Even the dry *rieslings* have a touch more body and richness; the more old-fashioned Pfalz wines have a weight and earthiness of their own. Underrated.

NAHE

Fruit-salad bouquet; firm, medium-light, crisp-bodied. Can be quite dry. Halfway, geographically and in style, between the Rheingau and Mosel.

MOSEL/SAAR/RUWER

Usually pale, green-tinged and often *spritzig* (very slight effervescence); fruity, light, high-toned *riesling* aroma; dry to medium-dry, usually light, low in alcohol, but enormously appealing with its characteristic refreshing acidity. In exceptional years, *Beerenauslese* and *Trockenbeerenauslese* quality wines can be made.

In essence, both Saar and Ruwer are mosel in style. Special characteristics: peach-like bouquet; often very dry and with fine, steely acidity, delicacy and subtlety. Thin, verging on tartness in lesser years.

BADEN

To the east of Alsace, Baden produces a large quantity of wine, both commercial and good, though rarely of fine quality. Rather foursquare in style; agreeable bouquet and flavour but relatively undistinguished, unsubtle and lacking zest. The reds are not very deep in colour, lacking the character and firmness of their French counterparts.

FRANCONIA (WÜRZBURG)

Known generally as Steinwein: fine, dry, steely wines from Würzburg, like *grand cru* chablis, yet with Germanic fruit and acidity. *Sylvaner* thrives here, producing wines of unusual firmness and quality.

——— **German vintages** ———

Great: 1945, 1949, 1953, 1959, 1971, 1989, 1990. *Very good:* 1947, 1964, 1975, 1976, 1988. *Good:* 1952, 1966, 1967, 1979, 1983, 1985, 1993, 1994. *Variable:* 1955, 1961, 1970, 1973, 1978, 1981, 1982, 1986, 1991, 1992. *Poor:* 1984, 1987.

AUSTRIA

Although there is a family resemblance, it is a mistake to compare Austrian whites with German Rhine wines. They look similar, have variations of a delicate grapey bouquet and are lightish in style but soft-edged, the fine wines lacking that distinguishing fruity-acidity and length. The *grüner veltliner* grape grown in the Wachau district typifies the soft, easy Austrian style. *Beeren* and *Trockenbeerenauslesen* dessert wines are made, but again, though good, often lack the length and breed of the German counterpart.

There are some top-class individual growers and commercial firms. Despite recent problems, the wines are worthy of attention, and good value.

HUNGARY

This once most characterful and varied wine country is now dominated by cooperatives and State marketing. Doubtless overall quality has improved; certainly the wines are good value. The range of table wines is far wider than in Austria; the whites are best though the highest quality officially encouraged is the equivalent of *Spät-auslese*. Look for softness, almost milkiness of bouquet and flavour. The famous reds from Eger are robust and assertive but lack finesse – ideal for paprika dishes.

TOKAY

This area stands out; it is one of the unique classic wine areas of the world.

● *Szamorodni*: the natural white wine of the region. Pale yellow in colour, characteristic appley nose of the *fürmint* grape, either quite dry or slightly sweet. Unusual flavour, fullish, quite good length.

● *Aszu*: ranges in colour from straw to deep yellow, golden-tinged with age. Pronounced appley nose, unlike any other wine aroma. Graduations of sweetness from two *puttonyos* slightly sweet, three '*putts*' roughly medium-sweet, four and five '*putts*' rich dessert wines. Fairly full-bodied but not heavy; rich, attractive spicy-straw flavour, good acidity and finish.

● *Essence*: no longer made for sale though an *aszu-essencia*, somewhat on a par with the former six *puttonyos*, is now marketed. Like a rich *aszu* but more luscious.

Tokay essence of old vintages varies from deep amber to deep tawny and has a very heavy sediment; a magnificent concentrated, raisiny, almost pungent nose (a cross between old Malmsey and a *Trockenbeerenauslese*); very sweet on the palate, rich, concentrated, with high acidity and a penetrating, lingering flavour and aromatic aftertaste. Appears to have unlimited life.

SWITZERLAND

There are three main areas, the Suisse-Romande, the German-speaking areas and the Italian-speaking areas. They produce a variety of reds and whites, ranging from commercial to moderately good; for local drinking rather than for export.

In the Suisse-Romande, the best reds, made from the *pinot noir* grown on the chalky soil of the upper Rhône, are soft, mild and of a burgundy character. The whites, from the *chasselas* grown on the shores of Lac Leman are often rather yellow, have fruit but tend to lack zest.

Reds from the German-speaking areas are generally light and unimpressive; the whites, from the *riesling* and *Müller-Thurgau* grapes are fresh and pleasant for early drinking.

The Italian-speaking areas produce wines of little interest except for a pleasant, rather mild *merlot* from the canton of Tessin (Ticino).

ITALY

An immense range of wines: all shades of colour, type and strength. Although quality can be high, connoisseurs' interest tends to be local except for the universally acknowledged classics.

CHIANTI

Made from four grapes, the balance, as in bordeaux, can vary from district to district and year to year. What are the distinguishing features? First, a rich garnet hue, deep when young, warm brick-red when mature; second, a deep, slightly earthy and complex flavour with a characteristic upturned finish: tannic and slightly bitter.

——————————— **Chianti vintages** ———————————
Great: 1962, 1964, 1967, 1971, 1975, 1978, 1985, 1988, 1990. *Very good:* 1955, 1957, 1968, 1974, 1977, 1979, 1986, 1994. *Quite good:* 1959, 1969, 1970, 1973, 1981, 1982, 1983, 1993. *Variable:* 1966, 1980, 1984, 1987, 1991, 1992.

BRUNELLO

Brunello di Montalcino is widely regarded as one of the greatest Italian reds. Of the Chianti family, but very deep brown-purple in colour, a hot concentrated aroma and flavour and swingeing finish. Immense keeping power and longevity. Expensive.

BAROLO

Perhaps the favourite amongst English connoisseurs, possibly because it is nearest to their idea of a classic red. Characteristics: fine deep colour, fruit and finesse on nose and palate; full-bodied yet finely balanced. Tannic when young, needs ageing, keeps well.

——————————— **Barolo vintages** ———————————
Great: 1961, 1964, 1971, 1978, 1982, 1985, 1988, 1990. *Very good:* 1967, 1970, 1979, 1986, 1989. *Good:* 1955, 1957, 1965, 1974, 1983. *Average:* 1959, 1962, 1966, 1968, 1969, 1973, 1975, 1976, 1981, 1994. *Variable:* 1980, 1991, 1992, 1993.

VALPOLICELLA

A lighter, elegant red from near Verona.

SOAVE

One of the best-known dry whites. They used to be yellow and flat owing to overmaturing in cask. Now they are fresher and altogether more pleasant and reliable.

MARSALA

One of the classic fortified wines of the world; deep, plummy-purple when young; sweet, meaty, almost malty nose; very sweet, full, rich, earthy-volcanic burnt flavour, with a tangy acid, sometimes slightly bitter, finish.

PORTUGAL

A wide range of table wines, many with character and above-ordinary quality. The reds are particularly interesting and are well-made and of good value. The whites vary from the light refreshing vinho verdes to the strange *madura* (mature) wines little seen outside the country, and perhaps as well, with some innocuous commercial dry whites in between.

Minho

Vinho verde can be white or red. Both are light, with slight to marked effervescent prickle and very high acidity that can be thin, even tart in the wrong context. Commercial wines are slightly sweeter, acidity toned down. The raw reds are rarely exported.

Dão

Reliable reds and whites. The best red Dão is full in colour and body, with positive bouquet – classic, but a little earthy – and fine flavour and finish. The whites are dry, sound but rather dull and lacking character.

Bairrada

The newest delimited region producing very dependable red wine. Always excellent value.

Setúbal

The Moscatel de Setúbal is a classic grapey dessert wine. Pale tawny-brown in colour; light, clear muscatel-grape aroma and flavour; sweet, of course, but not heavy in style.

PORT

All port is fortified with brandy, full-bodied and with a high alcoholic content. Red port is sweet, white is dryish. These are the main styles:

Ruby Should be full and true ruby in colour; fruity, peppery nose, not unlike young vintage port; invariably sweet, full and fruity. Tends to be strapping and hefty.

Tawny A true tawny, aged in the wood, is surprisingly pale in colour with an attractive amber-tawny hue and positive, sometimes lemon-yellow, rim; its next most noticeable feature is the soft nutty bouquet – sweet and harmonious. Invariably sweet on the palate but not heavy, indeed usually lightish, with gently rich, soft but nutty, extended flavour, and fine aftertaste. Lesser tawnies are far less distinctive.

White Palish, yellow-tinged; nose somewhat characterless; rarely truly dry, usually medium-dry and a trifle heavy and unexciting. Pleasant though lacking the freshness of sherry and the rich tang of a dry madeira. Serve very cold.

Vintage port Bottled two years after the vintage and matured in bottle. Modulations depend on the vintage, age and shipper's house style; quality is reliably high amongst the major port houses.

Young vintage port is deep, very purple, often opaque; rather peppery, alcoholic and unyielding on the nose; sweet, very full-bodied, fruity but slightly rasping.

Mature vintage port will have shed its colour and become medium-deep, much more tawny-hued; the bouquet will have ripened and developed overtones, sometimes liquorice-like. When very old the fruit fades leaving the brandy exposed. The maturing wine dries out, becoming lighter in body, softer and more harmonious.

Styles range from Noval – generally soft, light, feminine and forward – to Taylor – full, with firm backbone, great power, depth and longevity. Other classic vintage port *marques* include Cockburn, Croft, Dow, Fonseca, Graham, Sandeman and Warre.

────── **Port vintages** ──────
Great: 1945, 1955, 1963, 1966, 1977, 1985. *Very good:* 1947, 1948, 1960, 1970, 1983, 1991, 1992. *Good:* 1958, 1975, 1980, 1982, 1994. *Quite good:* 1950, 1967.

────── **Maturity span** ──────
Great classics: 12 to 80 years, at peak 15 to 40. *Good vintages:* 10 to 30 years.

MADEIRA

One of the three really great and traditional fortified wines of the world. Range: fairly dry to very sweet. Essential characteristics: rich burnt-tangy bouquet and flavour, and fairly high acidity. The rare top-quality wines have remarkable longevity. Commercial blends can be dull. Basic styles are named after grape varieties.

Sercial The palest, deep fino yellow, sometimes amber; the freshest, most mouth-watering aroma, but still with burnt-tangy character; dry to medium-dry, the lightest, but still with a fair amount of body.

Verdelho Varying amber-brown shades; nose deeper, richer, more tangy; medium-dry to medium-sweet, medium-full bodied, fairly rich attractive zestful wine with good acidity.

Bual Deeper, warm oloroso-type amber-brown; rich, more volcanic, meaty and assertive madeira tang; sweet, rich, fine-flavoured.

Malmsey Like Bual but sweeter and softer, with a rather more grapey-rich flavour added to the burnt-volcanic character. Intensely rich and attractive.

────── **Old vintage and old solera** ──────
The many authentic old solera and vintage madeiras have a common denominator: great richness of colour, powerful bouquet and length of flavour. A true old madeira has a positive tawny-brown colour with ruddy hue in the middle and pronounced greeny-amber rim; strong burnt aroma, high acidity; sometimes sweetness fades, but maintains a rich, complex flavour, concentrated, with extraordinarily powerful tang and extended finish.

Longest living after Tokay essence: often still full of character after 100 years or more.

SPAIN

The mass of Spanish table wine, red and white, is of ordinary to good commercial quality. Reds range from light to fairly full; whites are less appealing, the aroma of some being positively unattractive. Few will engage the attention of the connoisseur, though some do deserve it.

RIOJA AND PENEDES

Rioja is the major region producing wines of quality and style, particularly the reds which are of bordeaux type but often more supple and attractive than all but the best young claret. Fairly deep in colour; agreeable, fruity, sometimes classic, almost cedary, aroma; dry but not overtannic, pleasant medium-weight, soft through caskage; fine balance and flavour.

In Penedès a family firm, Torres, is making outstandingly good and moderately priced wines, both red and white.

SHERRY

Basically dry white wine, but with a wide range of styles within the two basic families: fino and oloroso. The former are usually dry and the latter, though starting dry, generally have sweetening wine blended in.

Fino Characteristics: paleness of colour, fine lemon straw-yellow; refined, positive, mouthwatering and distinctive *flor* aroma (less marked on lower quality wines); dry, light, fresh, with long crisp finish. Not very alcoholic.

Manzanilla A fino from Sanlúcar, usually very dry and with a fine tangy, almost salty, flavour.

Amontillado Deeper in colour; light amber-brown. Fine quality amontillados have a very slight fino-reminiscent smell but are richer and distinctly nutty. Dry to medium-dry, slightly fuller in body and nutty flavoured.

Palo Cortado A rarer and refined version of amontillado: similar colour and weight; dryish but a certain richness, nuttiness, vinosity and length of flavour.

Oloroso Total contrast to fino: deeper in colour, ranging from deep amber to warm amber-brown; complete absence of *flor* tang; softer, richer on nose and palate. The best are unsweetened, most are sweet. Medium to full-bodied.

Cream Commercial version of oloroso, sometimes paler; certainly very sweet and soft.

Brown Now almost totally out of fashion. Deep and brown coloured, with a burnt oloroso aroma; very sweet, heavy.

Pedro Ximenez The ultimate brown sherry: opaque; powerful, tangy, burnt-grapes aroma; very sweet, heavy, highly concentrated but fine acidity. Magnificent in its way but rarely seen.

UNITED STATES

Once condescendingly known as domestic and lacking the snob appeal of imported wines, the tables have turned. The development over the past 20 years has been astonishing.

CALIFORNIA

The scale, variety and quality of Californian wines are not to be underestimated: red, white, rosé, sparkling, fortified and flavoured; mass-produced, sound, commercial, refined, even rarefied. Amongst the fine wines, grape variety takes precedence over area. Even though the Napa Valley is undoubtedly the Mecca, other districts are also known to possess actual or potential classic vineyards. The wine-maker is all-important.

Cabernet Sauvignon The finest red, widely planted. Tends to be used alone, unblended. Characteristics: more consistently deep-coloured than in Bordeaux, often opaque and very purple when young, maintains its depth of colour better than claret with age; often a pronounced blackcurrant, recognizably *cabernet*, aroma but with earthy-volcanic overtones; slightly less dry than claret, often full-bodied, hefty wines full of fruit, rich in iron and quite tannic. Can be magnificent; long lasting.

Zinfandel Unique to California: variable, but mainly satisfactory fruity red, not unlike *cabernet* in weight, character and longevity. Possibly nearest to a Borolo in style.

Pinot Noir Not to be compared with burgundy. *Pinot noir* in California produces a deepish-coloured, full-bodied, rich, rounded wine. Most are devoid of the classic *pinot* aroma and flavour; some are remarkably good examples of the varietal.

Chardonnay Outstandingly the most successful varietal in terms of true classic style and quality. Colour ranges from palish to buttercup-yellow; remarkable *chardonnay* aroma: oak-vanilla tang, richness and freshness; dry to medium-dry. The old style more like a Corton-Charlemagne or Bâtard-Montrachet in weight. A move towards lighter, chablis-character wines is discernible. The best have a remarkably clean, true varietal flavour and quality, length and aftertaste.

Riesling Palish, fairly fruity, medium-dry and of general Germanic character but often lacking the inimitable freshness and light fruity-acidity of a Mosel. However, some outstanding sweet wines are now being made with late-picked and *botrytis*-induced grapes up to finest *Beerenauslese* quality. Also excellent Eiswein.

Fumé Blanc Although not absolutely comparable with the light acidic *blanc fumé* of the Loire, there are some consistently successful versions: pale; refreshing, fruity aroma; dry, appetizing and with crisp finish.

Sauvignon Blanc Synonym for *fumé blanc*.

Gewurztraminer Some of the spiciness and softness of the Alsace prototype but lacking complexity and delicacy.

— **Napa vintages** —

Great; 1946, 1951, 1958, 1965, 1968, 1985. *Very good:* 1947, 1956, 1964, 1966, 1969, 1970, 1973, 1978, 1980, 1982, 1991, 1992. *Good:* 1960, 1961, 1967, 1971, 1972, 1975, 1976, 1979, 1984, 1986. *Variable:* 1977, 1981, 1983, 1987, 1988–90, 1993, 1994.

OREGON AND WASHINGTON STATE

The cooler regions to the north of California are now producing excellent wines, notably *rieslings* and *pinot noir* with remarkable varietal character and quality.

NEW YORK STATE

Originally the home of jammy, boiled-sweet-like wines made from native American vines and hybrids. At one time the only light in this wilderness was provided by a remarkable grower and wine-maker, the late Dr Konstantin Frank. Other *vinifera* growers followed suit and some excellent pure wines are now being made, notably *rieslings* and *chardonnays*.

AUSTRALIA

To the older generation of Englishmen, Australian wine conjures up an iron-tonic burgundy-type wine sold in flagons.

The scene in Australia is totally different, the technology and enthusiasm resembling those of California but with far older traditions.

The range of styles and qualities is enormous. The practice of many big commercial firms, as well as small wineries, to produce a wide range, blending from different grapes and different regions, adds to the profusion – and confusion – of nomenclature.

HUNTER VALLEY

Perhaps the oldest classic district, in New South Wales, north of Sydney. The home of the *shiraz*, producing a rich, earthy burgundy/Rhône-style wine with the most evocative of all aromas: 'sweaty saddle'; also of the *semillon*, less interesting dry whites, and, a more recent development, of *chardonnay*. Good and big producers include McWilliams and the ubiquitous Lindeman's. Rothbury sets the pace, Tyrell the standards. Large and commercially successful is the Rosemount Estate, producing excellent *chardonnays*.

BAROSSA

A vast, broad, vine-clad valley in South Australia, north of Adelaide, with long-established family businesses like Yalumba and precociously successful newcomers like Wolf Blass; the enormous Kaiserstuhl cooperative (excellent *rieslings*); Seppeltsfield (fortified wines); and Orlando (producing *rieslings* of outstanding quality).

CLARE/WATERVALE

Also north of Adelaide, growing *cabernet*, *shiraz*, *rieslings*, and making good *flor* sherries. Wineries include Quelltaler, Chateau Clare, Stanley Leasingham and the tiny Sevenhills.

ADELAIDE
AND SOUTHERN VALES

Just surviving, in a suburb, is one of the great classic vineyards of Australia: Grange, whose Hermitage is deep, rich and magnificent, the Latour of the southern hemisphere. To the south of Adelaide are small family wineries like D'Arenberg Osborne and Kay's Amery; and large wineries like Seaview, Hardy's (magnificent ports) and the old Chateau Reynella, all producing a wide range of wines. Outstanding amongst the new wineries is Brian Croser's Petaluma.

COONAWARRA

An extraordinary strip of red earth in the middle of nowhere, first planted early this century, only lately recognized as the 'Médoc' of Australia; magnificent *cabernets* and *shiraz* reds, some good *rieslings* produced by Wynn's, Brand's Laira winery and Redman's.

RUTHERGLEN AND NORTHEAST
VICTORIA

An old-established classic area making a variety of wines, but famed for its magnificent rich tangy muscats, the great classic dessert wines of Australia. Best producers include Morris's, Chambers' Rosewood, All Saints and Bailey's Bundarra. Browns at Milawa produce a fine range of table wines, including excellent *Rhine-rieslings* and *shiraz*. Chateau Tahbilk, nearer to Melbourne, is worthy of special mention: quaint old winery producing *marsanne, semillon, shiraz* and top-quality *cabernet sauvignon.*

MELBOURNE AND YARRA VALLEY

Old districts resuscitated and some superb wines being made, notably *pinot noir* and *chardonnay.* James Halliday's Coldstream Hills – leading the field.

SOUTH AFRICA

Perhaps the most beautiful of all winelands, the Cape, once the home of some very well-known dessert wines, went into a long decline and has only relatively recently pulled out. Its postwar reputation was built upon its excellent sherries but now many fine wines are being made – magnificent *rieslings* at Nederburg and interesting reds at individual estates. The most at-home white is the *steen,* steely, fine; and, of the reds, the *shiraz,* an unusual style, not unlike its Australian counterpart. *Cabernet* has started to achieve real distinction.

ENGLAND

The resurgence of English vineyards has been remarkable. Pioneered by Sir Guy Salisbury-Jones and Colonel and Mrs Gore-Browne in the 1950s, small vineyards now abound in southern England, the best sweeping from Norfolk in the east to Wiltshire in the west. Unfortunately, the main hazard for the English grower is still the weather: grapes rarely ripen fully.

Several early-ripening white grapes are grown amongst which *Müller-Thurgau* has been the most popular, also *seyval* or *seyve villard.* District styles have not yet clearly emerged, but top vineyards – making better and more interesting wines than many competitors in the Loire and other northerly European districts – include Lamberhurst, Barton Manor, Wootton, Adgestone, Carr Taylor and Tenterden.

-------------------------------- **Summary** --------------------------------
I should like to end by making four points: first, that wine lovers should deliberately broaden their sights; second, in doing so, they should make allowances for strange styles and flavours, and appreciate the context – for example, rich food and hot climate – that certain wines were made for and taste best in; third, as witnessed positively by Australia and California (and slightly negatively by Hungary), that wine is as good, and as fine, as the wine drinker requires it to be and will pay for (or the State will allow). Positive, active, articulate connoisseurship and enthusiasm, allied to thriving economies (which allow healthy discretionary incomes) encourage the wine-maker to make the best possible wine within natural limitations beyond his control. For, and this is the fourth point, with all the will in the world, *great* wines cannot be made in unsuitable areas, which is why the connoisseur always returns with added appreciation to the well-tried and long-established classics.

	VERY LIGHT	LIGHT	MEDIUM LIGHT
VERY DRY		*Muscadet* *Chablis* *Sancerre* **Manzanilla** *Pouilly-Blanc Fumé* *Champagne* Bourgeuil *Chinon* *Savennières*	
DRY	*Saar-Ruwer* Beaujolais *Vinho Verde*	*Saumur-Champigny* *Saumur* *Mâcon blanc* *Listrac* Mâcon rouge Rully Santenay *Beaujolais blanc* Gigondas Pomerol *Vouvray* Lirac Côtes de Ventoux	**Fino** *Steinwein (Würzburg)* *Puligny-Montrachet* Valpolicella *Nahe* *Chevalier-Montrachet* *Chassagne-Montrachet* *Nahe Spätlese* Montagny Moulis Provence rosé *Riesling (Alsace)* Mercurey *Steen (S. Africa)* *Fumé-blanc (USA)* *Tokay d'Alsace* *Pinot d'Alsace* Tavel rosé *Muscat d'Alsace* *Meursault* *Rheingau Kabinett and Spätlese*
MEDIUM DRY	*Mid-Mosel* Anjou rosé	*Mosel Spätlese*	*Rheinhessen Spätlese* *Austrian whites* *Rheingau Auslese*
MEDIUM SWEET	*Moscato d'Asti*	*Mosel Auslese* Bonnézeaux	*Rheinhessen Auslese* *Champagne demi-sec* *Vouvray demi-sec*
SWEET			*Coteaux du Layon* *Mosel Beerenauslese* *Mosel Trockenbeerenauslese*
VERY SWEET			

KEY TO TYPE FACES: Red wine, *White wine,* **Red fortified wine,**

MEDIUM	MEDIUM FULL	FULL BODIED
Château-Chalon	*St-Estèphe*	
Vin Jaune		Brunello
Provence (White)		
Volnay		
Bourg		
	Zinfandel	
	Pauillac	
Hermitage blanc		
Blaye Chianti		Barolo
Dão Beaune		
	Bâtard-Montrachet	
St-Julien Hermitage rouge		
Aloxe- Corton Pomerol		Côte-Rôtie
Tokay Szamorodni		Le Corton
Chambolle-Musigny	Cabernet Sauvignon (USA)	
	Colares Pommard	Cahors
Semillon (Australia) Morey St-Denis	Richebourg	
	Chardonnay (USA)	Le Chambertin
Margaux Echézeaux	Vougeot	
Graves	*Corton-Charlemagne*	
Rioja Nuits St-Georges		
Palo Cortado	Vosne-Romanée	
Graves (Red)	*Le Montrachet*	
Sylvaner d'Alsace	St-Emilion	
	Pinot (USA)	
	Shiraz (Australia) Châteauneuf-du-Pape	
Dão		
Château Grillet **Amontillado**	Pinotage (S. Africa)	
Gewürztraminer	***Sercial***	
Johannisberg riesling (USA)		
Palatinate Spätlese	**White Port**	
	Châteauneuf blanc	
	Verdelho	
Tokay 2 putts		
Palatinate Auslese		
	Vintage Port	
Tokay 3 putts		**Bual**
Rheingau Beerenauslese Barsac		**Oloroso**
Lunel		**Ruby Port**
Beaumes de Venise	**Muscat (Australia)**	
Muscat de Frontignan		**Marsala**
Tawny Port		
Rheinhessen Beerenauslese		
Moscatel de Setubal *Tokay 4 putts*		***Brown Sherry***
Palatinate Beerenauslese		
	Cream Sherry	
Rheingau Trockenbeerenauslese Sauternes		
Rheinhessen Trockenbeerenauslese		**Malmsey**
Palatinate Trockenbeerenauslese		**Pedro Ximenez**
	Tokay Essence	

White fortified and **liqueur wine**

IV

THE SENSES OF SIGHT, SMELL AND TASTE

Tasting is the introduction of wine to our senses:
sight, smell and taste.
Emile Peynaud

———————— **Sense of sight** ————————

Those fortunate to have eyesight employ this sense every minute of their waking day. Our eyes have plenty of practice. Even colour awareness, for example, which may not be as fully developed as an artist's, is normally at a high level, mainly because of constant use. The enormous advantage that colour has over smell and taste is that it can be so much more easily described, recorded or matched and conveyed from one person to another.★ In the last resort it can be accurately reproduced.

On the other hand, the senses of smell and taste are rarely so highly or so continuously employed. Indeed, the level of awareness can be abysmally low. This is partly owing to the fact that the sense of smell is easily fatigued (after only a short time a worker in a chocolate factory or a tannery does not notice the smell) and partly because it is less frequently exercised.

Flavour is a compound of taste and smell, yet although the sensitivity and selectivity of the latter sense is infinitely higher it is the least consciously applied. In relation to wine, most people 'taste' – in a superficially literal sense – but very few deliberately and consciously smell the wine first, let alone derive any positive information or pleasure from that act. What is far too little known is that a great deal of what one wants, or needs, to know about wine can be detected from its appearance and bouquet alone. The actual taste on the palate basically confirms the impressions that sight and smell have previously conveyed and adds to the sum total.

———————— **Sense of smell** ————————

Smell is perhaps the most basic and most primitive of all the senses; more than any other it invokes memory in a particularly direct manner. The 'smell-brain', with its direct contact with the memory areas, can act as an immediate catalyst to recognition and identification. This accounts for the value of the first impression that, justifiably, can be relied upon by experienced tasters.

Let me deal now in some detail with the mechanics of smell. Physically, this is what happens: the stimulus that excites the sense of smell results from certain substances, in solution, coming into contact with myriads of highly complex cells in the nose. Such substances usually enter the nose in the form of vapour. In the case of wine they are conveyed by volatile esters and aldehydes. At this stage they are taken over by the olfactory system. The first pair of cranial nerves are called olfactory nerves. They begin as specialized olfactory cells in the lining of

★A complete and universally accepted scientific analysis, classification and description of smells and tastes, despite a mass of multidisciplinary research and enquiries, appears to defy solution. Perhaps, slightly out of context, I can quote the last sentence of the epilogue of Dr Roland Harper's *Odour Description and Odour Classification*: 'Perhaps at present this remains more of an art than a science'.

the upper part of the nose. Fibrils from these cells pass up into the olfactory bulbs, lying in the base of the skull. From the bulbs the olfactory tracts – thick bands of white brain matter – pass backwards to enter the brain, and the fibres contained in the tracts are brought into relationship with nerve cells in certain parts of the brain. The original stimulus at the nerve endings is, in effect, converted into a sensation for the brain to interpret.

An interesting fact is that overprolonged exposure to one smell may reduce the effectiveness of that smell, but that other smells may be readily detected. From a practical point of view this means that it is pointless to sniff too long or too frequently at one wine. If the first impression is lost, it is probably better to move on to the next wine. Then move back to the original or tackle it again after a rest (*see also* pp. 107–08).

In my experience, passing one's nose over the glass and lightly inhaling will often yield virtually all the bouquet has to offer. Nevertheless, it is sensible to swirl the wine gently and smell it again more carefully. Sometimes it is necessary to sniff vigorously and inhale deeply either to determine whether there is fruit under the unyielding exterior or, perhaps, to isolate a fault in a poor wine.

Chambré-ing red wines or cupping the glass in one's hands has a good practical reason. There is evidence that whatever the state of the substance having smell, its appreciation depends on that substance passing into the solution with which the olfactory cells are normally bathed. But the higher the molecular weight of the wine, the greater the need to encourage the process of vaporization. This is accomplished by gently raising its temperature. When wine is warmed, convectional currents arise, moving the wine and releasing its bouquet.

A cold start accounts for the 'dumbness' of a massively constituted red wine, even if mature. It also accounts for the remarkable aftertaste and lingering farewell that arises from the naso-pharynx as the mouth-warmed wine passes down the throat and the released volatile esters rise through the back nasal passages.

Conversely, light wines, with low extract and weight do not need to be warmed. Those which are light but relatively high-toned (such as a mosel of a moderate year) will release bouquet with an impact that is immediate but which lacks depth. They rely not on an aftertaste but on a high degree of natural acidity to give the wine a finish – to which chilling adds crispness.

Some pungent substances have a more physical impact, stimulating the nerve endings in a tactile sense. For example, sulphur dioxide can be detected by a prickle in the nose even though its presence in the wine may not be strong enough to affect the olfactory system. Certain of the higher alcohols can also have a similar effect, producing a feeling rather than a smell. Acetic acid can be both felt and smelled.

Sense of taste

The sense of taste depends on the stimulation of organs known as taste buds. These are mainly situated in the tongue, though a few are found in the soft palate, and their sensitivity varies. The nerves connected with the taste buds carry impulses to the nerve centre in the medulla (which is the name for the marrow at the top of the spinal cord), whence they are carried to the parts of the brain towards the tip and inner sides of the temporal lobe – in close relation to the area of the brain concerned with the sense of smell.

To cause the necessary stimulus, a substance must be in solution and the sensation it evokes relates to one, or a combination, of the four so-called primary elements of taste*: sweetness (best appreciated at the tip of the tongue), sourness† (upper edges of the tongue), bitterness (at the back) and saltiness (at the sides).

If one understands which parts of the palate detect which basic tastes, it will be quite apparent that to peck at wine, i.e. to take a very small sip or leave only the tip of the tongue in contact, will not enable the taster to appreciate more than a fraction of the wine's physical characteristics. A reasonable mouthful must be taken and it must be swirled round the mouth so that all the taste buds can get to work on it. Some experienced tasters take a large mouthful and draw air across their palate, often with rather an off-putting guzzling noise. This distributes the wine across the whole of the palate and allows the volatile scents to ascend the back of the nose for the olfactory nerves to play their part.

A word of warning about a common problem which is rarely discussed by other tasters and yet one to which, I must confess, I am frequently susceptible. Beware of scalding the mouth with hot liquids; the wine will taste abnormally sharp due to the acidity biting the raw tongue.

Sense of touch

Tactile impressions, implying the use of fingers and hands, do not, strictly speaking, apply to the tasting process. Nevertheless, wine produces reactions which have certainly nothing to do with sight, smell or taste, and are as equally certainly tactile; for example, the weight (body) of wine in the mouth, the silkiness and velvety texture of certain wines, the evaluation of extract and components detected physically in the mouth, and the prickle of carbon dioxide (*spritzig*) in the lightly sparkling or fully sparkling state. Also certain chemical reactions in the mouth and nose affect the tactile sense more than the sense of smell. Sulphur dioxide, already mentioned, is an example.

Sense of hearing

The sense of hearing does not seriously enter into wine tasting. There is nothing like the delightful crunchiness of a crisp biscuit – unless it be the anticipatory pop of a cork, the sound of pouring and tinkling of glasses, the fizz of champagne or the ministering sizzle of Alka-Seltzer the following morning! As for those audible signs of approval, considered good manners at the Chinese dinner table, they have no part, whether involuntary or voluntary, in polite wine society.

Gastric stimulation

Before leaving the physical element of wine tasting, it is perhaps worth mentioning an important effect: the stimulation of the gastric juices. Quite apart from its health-giving natural properties, wine is a superlative aid to digestion. The appetite is whetted by the smell and taste of a refreshingly youthful white wine, and by the tingling dryness, the acidity and even the slight bitterness of many reds. The nerves of taste and smell are

---

*According to Dr Roland Harper, 'There is relatively little evidence to support the concept of primary tastes.' (*The Human Senses in Action*, 1972).
†Sourness, in a wine context, has a derogatory connotation. Acidity, an essential component, is the word English wine tasters use (*see* Chapter XII).

stimulated, which, in turn, increase the activity of the salivary glands. Also, through a reflex nervous action, the wine markedly increases the amount of digestive juice secreted in the walls of the stomach; it flows more rapidly, and the movements of the stomach are speeded up. This stimulation of the muscular wall of the stomach extends to that of the bowel, greatly aiding the digestion of the accompanying food.

But let us turn to the act of tasting. . . .

V
THE ELEMENTS OF TASTING

*Your true amateur sips his wine; as he lingers over each
separate mouthful, he obtains from each the sum total of pleasure
which he would have experienced had he emptied his
glass at a single draught.*

Brillat-Savarin
The Physiology of Taste, 1825

The order in which one tastes a wine is based on the natural
physical movement of the glass from table to mouth. First of all,
the glass is picked up and the wine is looked at. This is stage one.
As it is raised towards the mouth the nose catches the bouquet –
stage two. Then the lips meet the rim of the glass, and the literal
tasting, stage three, commences.

But, over and above this, there is a correlation between what
one sees, smells and tastes. The last tends to confirm visual and
nasal impressions. The logical conclusion is stage four, the
summary of overall impressions, and the final verdict.

Before starting, make sure that the glasses are suitable and the
lighting adequate.

Glasses

If you do not possess an ideal tasting glass just use a conventional, tulip-shaped, crystal-clear wine glass, *not* a fancy
or coloured one. An ideal tasting glass is one which conforms
to a specific design laid down by an international panel for
official standards organizations. Such a glass is illustrated on the
facing page. There are several acceptable variations on this
theme, but this is the glass which has been adopted by all the
major European institutions for use in recognized tasting
competitions.

If tasting a range of wines, use matching glasses of a generous
size and rinse them out with wine if they are at all musty or
unclean or if they have been previously washed with detergent.
Pour an equal measure in each so that the relative depth and hue
can be seen at a glance. Do not fill the glass more than half full, as
it will be easier to tilt above a white table top, an essential
manoeuvre if the informative colour at the rim of the wine is to
be seen clearly. It will also enable the wine to be swirled around
in the glass without spilling, collecting the volatile substances
prior to nosing.

Pick up the glass by its stem or foot, not by the bowl. This
makes it easier to examine the wine, particularly if held in front
of a lighted candle. It also avoids the influence of body warmth
and has the minor virtue of avoiding finger marks on the sides
of the glass. (Handling old bottles can be a dirty business; wine
itself tends to be sticky if dripping or spilt.)

Lighting

Daylight is best, preferably a good north light, as artificial
lighting can affect both hue and tone. In particular, avoid
fluorescent lighting; it makes red wine look unhealthily brown,
even blue-tinged. Candle light enhances the appearance of wine
but for a serious tasting the only benefit of a candle is to reveal
the true degree of clarity of the wine; thus it is useful in a cellar
when young wine is drawn from the cask, or when decanting a
bottle before dinner.

THE IDEAL TASTING GLASS

Diameter of open top
46 millimetres, plus or
minus 2

Overall height
155 millimetres, plus or
minus 5

Total capacity
215 millilitres, plus or
minus 10

Thickness of glass
0.8 millimetres, plus or
minus 0.1

Manufacture
Colourless transparent
crystal glass containing
about 9% lead

Height of bowl
100 millimetres, plus or
minus 2

Diameter at widest part
65 millimetres, plus or
minus 2

Tasting quantity
50 millilitres

**Height of base and
stem**
55 millimetres, plus or
minus 3

Thickness of stem
9 millimetres, plus or
minus 1

This is based on International
Standard ISO 3591-1977
reproduced with permission
of the International
Standards Organization. Full
details can be obtained from
the ISO and its member
bodies (in the U.K., the
British Standards Institution
specification is BS 5586)

Diameter of base
65 millimetres, plus or
minus 5

Temperature

Make sure the temperature of the wine is correct: room temperature for reds (including port), cold for rosé and white (around 45–50°F or 7–10°C). The actual room temperature will naturally vary from place to place and with the time of year. The range could well be anywhere between 60 and 65°F, 16 to 18°C.* Make sure the glasses for red wine are at the same temperature and not brought out of a cold cupboard at the last minute.

It is worth noting that dry white wines cool more quickly than sweet: sauternes needs more time in an ice-bucket, and sprinkling sea salt on the ice can be a very effective aid to cooling. But best of all, in my experience, is to have an ice-box or refrigerator at the right temperature and then transfer the wine to an open thermos flask. There is an excellent one on the market called Vinicool®.

Stage 1:

APPEARANCE

Under the heading of appearance,† the taster looks at three facets: colour, depth and clarity. As each of these facets is examined, the reader is advised to refer to the illustrated examples on pp. 81–96.

Colour or hue

Most table wines fall into one of three basic categories: red, white or rosé. Fortified wines vary: sherry is technically a white wine and ranges from pale straw-yellow to deep brown; port may be red or white, the former ranging from deep purple, ruby to pale tawny. Perhaps the main thing to bear in mind is that the colour should be appropriate for the type and age of wine.

Red wines

What we call a *red* wine will, in fact, vary in hue from deep purple through various shades of red to mahogany or even amber, depending mainly on its state of maturity, the vintage and the district. The length of fermentation and the time the grape juice is kept on the skins have a major influence, as does the time kept in cask. The red colour comes from a group of pigments called anthocyanins extracted from the grape skins by the action of alcohol. Different grape species have varying types of anthocyanins. These free anthocyanins provide most of the (purple) colour of young wine but, in effect, they fade or merge into larger tannin molecules which combine with the anthocyanins to change the colour, to red, then red-brown as the wine ages. Oxidation speeds up this process. Dead colouring matter is precipitated and forms part of the sediment of an old wine.

Purple Indicates extreme youth and/or immaturity. Almost all young red wine in cask will have this colour. The time taken in bottle to lose its strong purple tinge depends on the initial depth of colour.

Ruby Self-descriptive. The colour of a young port or a deepish claret or burgundy, having lost its pristine flush of purple.

---

*Professor Peynaud's ideal tasting room is 65°F or 18°C with 60% humidity.
†I use the term in its broadest sense: that which is perceived by the eye, and not in a limited sense like 'clarity'.

Red In vinous terms red is the colour approximating to 'claret'. It indicates the transitional period between youth and the acquisition of maturity and bottle-age. The lower the pH the greater the amount of active pigments and the higher the intensity of colour. A particularly intense red is, therefore, often indicative of high acid content. Max Léglise calls **cherry red** the 'cruising' colour of a wine in perfect health in its fruit aroma stage.

Red-brown In a table wine this hue indicates maturity (for example, claret with five years or more in bottle, burgundy three years or more – depending on the weight and quality of the vintage). A brown tinge can also result from baked vines after a hot summer, also from artificially heated and 'cooked' wine (i.e. during fermentation), or from oxidation owing to overexposure to air in cask.

Mahogany A more mellow, subtle red-brown indicating maturity (claret with 10 to 20 years bottle-age, burgundy of a moderate vintage with over 10 years' bottle-age).

Tawny A term, like ruby, usually associated with port. It describes a hue that has been attained through loss of colour over a period of years in cask, a natural but expensive maturing process. Cheap commercial tawnies are made by blending white wines with red.

Amber-brown Indicates either a wine of very considerable age or one which is prematurely old and/or oxidized. Once the remaining healthy ruddy glow fades away the wine is usually dead.

--------- *White wines* ---------

White wines range from virtual colourlessness through the palest yellow-green and deeper shades of yellow, to gold and deep amber brown.

Dry white wines usually start off life pale in colour, and, unlike red wines, slowly gain colour with age. Sweet wines generally start off a deeper shade of yellow, turn to gold and then take on an amber-brown tinge with age. Phenolic compounds provide the yellow pigment of young white wines and these vary according to the grape used (for example, low in *rieslings*) and wine-making methods. Higher phenolics can be produced by grape ripeness, by skins affected with *botrytis* producing the yellow-gold of young sauternes and *Trockenbeerenauslesen*, by the length of time the young wine spends in wooden casks, and the type of wood used.

Young natural sherry is basically a pale straw-yellow, the deeper shades being the result of ageing and/or blending. Practically all the dark oloroso and brown sherries gain their colour from added *color* wine of one sort or another.

Pale yellow-green A distinct green tinge is quite common in youthful white wines, due to residual chlorophyll, and is a particular, if not essential, characteristic of a chablis or a young mosel. It is rarely seen in the white wines made in hot climates.

Straw-yellow A pleasant lively colour common to the majority of white wines, particularly the drier ones. In Burgundy, Meursault tends to be more yellow than Montrachet, and in Alsace, *traminer* more yellow than *riesling*, though this cannot be relied on.

Yellow-gold An abnormal colour for a young dry white wine but most frequently seen in the sweeter varieties, such as sauternes and high quality German dessert wines of *Beerenauslese* and *Trockenbeerenauslese* quality.

Gold Generally indicates either a lusciously sweet wine, or one with considerable bottle-age (for example, a white burgundy, usually pale straw when young, will develop a slight golden sheen after about six years in bottle).

Yellow-brown or old gold The colour of many dessert wines, fortified ones in particular. However, a brown or orange tinge in a white table wine indicates considerable bottle-age, overmaturity and other degrees of oxidation. Many white burgundies will take on an unhealthy brown tinge after about 12 years in bottle; yet a fine sauternes may not develop it for 30 years or more.

Maderized This word is used to describe the appearance and condition of overmaturity and oxidation. A maderized white wine presents a dull, drab appearance, with a pallid yellow-brown colour.

Brown Probably well past drinking (unless it is a sherry of that name or the tawny-brown of a very old port).

--------------- *Rosé wines* ---------------

Wines described as rosé can vary considerably in colour and depth. Each district has its own style, depending on the type of grape used and on the method of making. The better rosés are made from black grapes, the skins being left in contact with the fermenting grape juice just long enough for red pigment to be extracted. Cheap rosés are sometimes a blend of red and white wines. Some commercial blends of pink champagne are made by adding red wine from the Montagnes de Reims.

The colour of a rosé is half its charm. A rosé wine is usually drunk young, for if allowed to age it would lose its freshness of colour and taste. Some rosés begin life the colour of onion skin, a characteristic of those wines appropriately termed *pélure d'oignon* and *vin gris*.

Rosé The perfect rosé should not look like a watered-down red wine, nor should it support an excess of orange or purple. It should be positive, bright and appealing.

Orange Some grape varieties produce a distinct orange tint. Pure orange is not a desirable hue although a pleasant orange-pink is quite normal and characteristic of many rosés from the Loire. Orange is often more marked in Provence and the hot south.

Pink A self-descriptive hue, suggestive of artificiality. Any suspicion of a blue tinge indicates unhealthiness, probably from bad fining or some contamination.

--------------- **Depth of colour** ---------------

Although the basic deepness or paleness of a wine depends to a certain extent on its origin, the relative depth of colour will give a good indication of its physical content.

It is sometimes difficult to judge the comparative depth of colour of two wines. One method is to fill each of the glasses to the same height, place them side by side and look at each from a position vertically above; alternatively arrange a light behind the glasses and compare the relative depth of colour of the shadow cast by each wine on a white table top, a little-known but very effective way for all colours of wine.

--------------- **Red wines** ---------------

Depth, in association with the actual colour or hue, will also give an indication of the age and maturity of a red wine. For example, a very deep, nearly opaque, red-purple wine will almost certainly have more than its fair share of tannins and other natural components. A colour like this will only be seen in a well-made wine of a fine vintage, its properties being derived from rich, fully ripe grapes with sun-thickened skins. The converse applies equally: a pale red wine results from too high a yield per hectare, from hasty vinification, or a poor year in which the grapes have failed to mature and whose skins are thin and deficient in pigment.

As red wine matures, colouring matter is deposited. The wine becomes less deep, eventually pale and faded.

White wines

Depth of colour is relatively unimportant in young dry white wines. The variations are comparatively small and the connotations usually inconclusive. A very pale mosel, for example, is likely to be neither better nor worse than one which is medium-pale. White wines tend to deepen with bottle-age. This is due to phenolic molecules joining together, the larger molecules having deeper amber-gold and brown colours. Oxidation speeds up the process.

The depth of colour of sweet white wines is more meaningful. Care must be taken not to confuse the deep gold of an old sauternes of a great vintage with maderization. Château d'Yquem of the 1921 and 1929 vintages is very deep – deep gold, not deep brown – indicative of the extraordinarily high initial sugar content and extract. The point is that these vintages were deep in colour when young. Beware also of drawing a wrong conclusion from a *pale* old sauternes. This is indicative of either a lesser vintage and/or over-sulphuring prior to bottling. The latter acts as a preservative, inhibiting development and colour change. The use of steel vats rather than wood also tends to reduce the colour.

Clarity

This is of prime importance in the various stages of development of all wines from the time of fermentation, during cask life, through to the time of bottling.* Thereafter, white wines should be star-bright and trouble-free. Red wines are normally expected to throw a sediment in bottle. Fine wines often have extra lustre and luminosity.

The clarity of wine is best judged by holding the glass in front of a candle or some other bright light.

Upper surface The upper surface of the wine in the glass is worth inspection. It should of course be bright. If it appears dull, iridescent or bitty, trouble may be indicated. With very old wine, I also look out for the tell-tale bead of persistent small bubbles around the meniscus which generally gives advance warning that the wine is cracking up.

Cloudiness Hold up the glass to the light, or against a candle. A dull cloudiness or obstinate haze of suspended matter in bottled wine is a bad sign; in normal circumstances, the wine should

---

*The rather attractive silver *tastevins* which are sold in Burgundian souvenir shops (and used by tourists as ashtrays) are, in fact, traditional tasting vessels with a peculiar usefulness. The circular indentations in the shallow sides reflect candle light across the metal base to reveal at a glance in an ill-lit cellar the clarity of the new wine drawn from the cask. A *tastevin* is also more portable and less fragile than a glass though it is somewhat pretentious to take one to a normal tasting; a proper tasting glass is more useful. (In the Burgundy and Beaujolais regions the *tastevin* also has symbolic guild connotations.)

be returned to the supplier. A permanent cloudiness or dull opacity is due to metallic contamination, usually copper or iron *casses*, or yeasts. Incidentally, think carefully before condemning a cloudy *red* wine. Was it recently delivered or carried up from the cellar hastily and clumsily? Old vintage port usually has a heavy sediment or crust and even when carefully decanted may still have 'fliers' or 'beeswing' (very descriptive) in it. The latter are normal (and tasteless) and can be ignored.

Cork, not corked Tiny pieces of floating cork are harmless; so are most forms of sediment which settle easily in the bottle. Bits of cork in the wine may be due to a bad corking machine or, more usually, to the careless use of a poor corkscrew. Wine with cork floating on it is *not* corked – an ignorant misunderstanding in restaurants which can lead to fatuous and unnecessary complaints. Just pick the cork out.

Crystals Flakes of tartaric acid crystals are sometimes seen in fortified wine and white table wine. They have usually been caused by a sudden fall in temperature. These flakes or crystals generally settle quickly, are quite harmless and do not impair the flavour of the wine.

Limpidity It is an appropriate phenomenon that a really beautiful limpid colour is often indicative of a really fine wine whereas an ordinary blended wine will often have a dull nondescript lack-lustre appearance.

Grades of clarity shade down from brilliant, star-bright, bright and clear to dull, bitty, hazy and cloudy.

Intensity Last but not least the intensity of colour, by which I mean the strength of colour at the rim, as opposed to the more usual tailing off to a watery edge, is, in relation to red wines and old fortified wines in particular, an indication of quality, strength, extract.

Legs or tears I have never been a 'leg' man myself; indeed, there seems to be some confusion over the term in relation to wine. Full-bodied wines, those with high extract and alcohol content form 'legs' or 'tears' – globules with extended tails – which fall slowly to the surface of the wine after the glass has been swirled. This can, with some justification, be considered to presage richness, but I personally prefer to rely on my palate. Incidentally, carelessly washed and dried glasses can play havoc with the meniscus. 'Legs' can also be created by the surface tension pump which is due to the evaporation of ethyl alcohol at the meniscus or rim which mysteriously draws up a small quantity of wine.

Level or ullage

Although this relates to the appearance of wine in the bottle rather than in the glass, it is appropriate to refer to it here. A lower level than normal can be due to:

Short fill The result of sloppy bottling and careless inspection; level low neck or around upper shoulder. Usually little to worry about.

Reduction A natural contraction* which can occur in bottle over a period of time. In my experience mature burgundies can show a 4·5 to 7 cm ullage without deleterious effect.

Cork failure The commonest cause of ullage is cork failure due to cork weevil or lack of springiness due to old age. Cork weevil

---

*I understand that if a gallon of water and a gallon of alcohol are mixed, the combined total measures less than two gallons.

is not uncommon, particularly in badly maintained private cellars. It is about the only thing which will affect the condition of old vintage port, particularly if the protective wax seal has broken or worn away: the weevil will bore holes in the cork and let air in. The wine will become acetic, or at least tainted.

Corks, like human bodies, eventually lose their suppleness and firmness with age. After 20 years or so, the elasticity of cork weakens, though high-quality long claret corks can protect wine for a century. Uneven ullages, quite common with very old wine, are almost always due to cork failure. Recorking – standard practice in the great châteaux and domaine cellars – is the answer. Failing this (as with the great Rosebery pre-phylloxera clarets) regular waxing of seals and capsules, whilst otherwise remaining unmoved in a cold slightly damp cellar, will preserve the corks and wine.

Ullaged bottles *can* turn out surprisingly well. Sometimes the air in the space does not harm the wine. If the cork is not foul, and the colour of the wine deep and good, the wine, even though old and vulnerable, may miraculously survive. But it must be of high quality to begin with.*

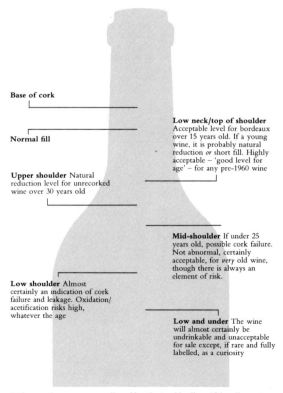

Base of cork

Normal fill

Upper shoulder Natural reduction level for unrecorked wine over 30 years old

Low neck/top of shoulder Acceptable level for bordeaux over 15 years old. If a young wine, it is probably natural reduction *or* short fill. Highly acceptable – 'good level for age' – for any pre-1960 wine

Mid-shoulder If under 25 years old, possible cork failure. Not abnormal, certainly acceptable, for *very* old wine, though there is always an element of risk.

Low shoulder Almost certainly an indication of cork failure and leakage. Oxidation/acetification risks high, whatever the age

Low and under The wine will almost certainly be undrinkable and unacceptable for sale except, if rare and fully labelled, as a curiosity

*I frequently come across ullaged bottles in old cellars. If the ullages, in a bin-full of one wine, are fairly uniform, and the corks and caps appear sound, I do not worry overmuch.

Old champagne can look ullaged, but if the cork and foil are sound this ullage generally turns out to be carbon dioxide out of solution. No longer bubbly, the champagne will have turned into a calm, golden-sheened wine much beloved of English connoisseurs, somewhat to the exasperation of the French.

Stage 2:

NOSE OR BOUQUET

The importance and value of nosing a wine are generally underrated, for a great deal of valuable information about any wine may be gained from the smell alone. The first impression is generally the most telling. The more mature the wine, the more important the nose becomes.

The best procedure is to take hold of the stem of the glass lightly and, keeping its base on the table, rotate it briskly. This exposes the maximum surface area of wine, encouraging the release by vaporization of its esters. It also neutralizes the smell of a dirty glass.

Bring the glass to the nose and concentrate on the first fleeting impression. Is it clean and fresh? Are there any very positive characteristics: the grape aroma, high mouth-watering acidity, etc.? Next, give the glass another swirl and give a number of short sharp sniffs. This will reveal depths of fruit and other salient features not, perhaps, noticed at first. I do *not* recommend very deep inhalation: this merely deadens the senses.★

The smell of wine can be of two types: that which reminds one of another smell, or one that is, with experience, recognizable as a more-or-less pure chemical substance or compound. In essence, however, the wine taster has to learn to detect and recognize different grape aromas, youthfulness and maturity, pure wine scents and, with more experience, complex overtones.

It is difficult enough to analyse and describe most common-or-garden smells; even more so the subtleties of a refined bouquet. And if it is difficult to pin down the elements of bouquet, it is almost impossible to convey them to another person. Some of the characteristics are obvious and easily describable, some can only be recognized by an experienced nose. The following facets should be examined, preferably in this order:

Cleanliness

Basically what is meant is that the wine should smell like wine, pure and unencumbered. Anything redolent of bad cabbages, old socks, vinegar, almond kernels, pear drops or any clearly extraneous or foreign smells, should be regarded as suspect, to say the least. In practice this is an automatic reflex action.

Sulphur dioxide, quite common on European white wines (it is reminiscent of burnt match sticks or the whiff of a coke oven), is regarded as more of a nuisance than an off-smell. Aeration, decanting and swirling in the glass all lessen the effect. If no off-odours are readily apparent one passes on to the more positive wine smells.

Grape variety

The experienced taster will next look out for the first major clue

★The late Allan Sichel favoured 'short sharp sniffs with his mouth open'. Frankly, I find this does not work for me with wine, although I have recently discovered that it is very effective for smelling brandy which, with nose alone, so often gives a too sharply spirity impression.

to the origin of the wine: the characteristic grape aroma.★ The classic noble vines, *cabernet sauvignon*, *pinot*, *riesling*, *traminer* and so on, produce their own individual aromas. However, even these are not always easy to detect, and the only way to memorize them is to taste and retaste first-rate examples until their characteristics are firmly lodged in the mind (*see* pp. 14–19 and glossary in Chapter XII).

Wines made from lesser grape varieties and from minor districts will less frequently produce a distinct and recognizable aroma. More often it will be just vaguely varietal, and if indistinguishable but pleasant will merely be described as vinous.

Youth, age and maturity

The age of a wine can be accurately judged on the nose by an experienced taster. It is not as difficult as it might appear at first and, as always, the comparison of good specimens of different vintages is the best way to learn.

The physical components of young wine tend to be pronounced and raw as they have had little time to settle down and blend together. Acidity in young wine has a mouth-watering effect. A raw cooking apple smell indicates excess malic acid and is frequently found in young, unripe white wines, particularly from poorer vintage years in northerly climes.

As the wine mellows with age, its bouquet★ becomes noticeably softer and more harmonious. It also develops what is known as 'bottle-age'. It is almost impossible to describe bottle-age; on most white wines this shows up as a honeyed quality; red wines become richer and deeper with bottle-age. Complex and harmonious are perhaps the operative words. A wine with too much bottle-age will show deterioration by taking on a flat, dull, toffee-like smell (maderized) or what is known as bottle-stink (oxidation, which can produce a smell like bad cabbages). The point is that bottle-age is all part of the maturing process that is revealed to the taster.

Fruit

Fruit is a desirable quality, but it should be noted that a wine can be described as fruity without having any trace of grapeyness. A distinctly grapey bouquet is only found in wines made from certain unmistakable grape varieties. High tannin content in a young red wine tends to mask the fruit.

Depth and intensity

A bouquet can be described as light or deep, intense, nondescript, superficial, full or rounded, depending on the development of the wine. However, care must be taken not to be misled by the 'full', i.e. fully developed bouquet of a mature but poor-quality wine or, conversely, by the 'dumb' or undeveloped bouquet of a high quality but immature wine.

It is hard to define quality. What one is looking for is an unfolding, an exposure of bouquet that is rich, many-faceted, but soft; forthcoming yet harmonious. And the bouquet of a *great* wine is not only overwhelmingly beautiful but tends to linger in the glass even when it has been drained to the last drop.

There are many conventional terms used to describe the bouquet of wine. The principal ones are defined in Chapter XII.

★The expressions 'aroma' and 'bouquet' are used in the senses defined in the glossary in Chapter XII. However, both are frequently muddled in usage.

Stage 3:

TASTE

The taste, or gustatory stage, should first and foremost confirm conclusions drawn from the appearance and bouquet. The palate is a fairly basic evaluator. In fact it provides the taster with rather less information than the eye and nose, unless the wine is new in cask. The younger the wine, the more important the palate element becomes. This is not to suggest that taste is unimportant. Far from it. In any case a factor, excess acidity for example, not spotted by the nose may be detected on the palate: a sort of long-stop situation.

As indicated in Chapter IV, there are several points of oral contact which will reveal different taste characteristics. For this reason, one tiny sip is usually inadequate. Do not peck at the wine; take a reasonable mouthful, swirl it round the mouth; then, if at a tasting, spit it out and repeat the process if necessary.

Elements of taste

It is recommended that the elemental characteristics that are detected on the palate be noted in strict order. It matters less what the order is than that the order is a habitual one. In this way one avoids overlooking vital factors. Here are the basic movements and observations. Read through and then refer to Chapter XII.

Dryness and sweetness A basic and easily judged constituent, particularly important in white wines. Do not be misled by thinness or excessive acidity, which tend to make one underestimate the actual sugar content, and vice versa. There is also an apparent sweetness noticeable in hot-country wines and in the wines of particularly good vintages in northern Europe: in each case this derives from fully ripe grapes and from ethyl alcohol which has a slight sweetening effect.

Acidity Acidity is a major element in the make-up of any wine. It gives a wine purpose, life, zing and finish. I tend to think of acidity as the nervous system of a wine. Extremes of acidity are, however, undesirable. Excess sugar and glycerol, natural or otherwise, tend to mask the true degree of acidity.

The principal, and desirable, grape acidity in wine is tartaric. The most undesirable is acetic which when present in excess makes the wine taste vinegary.

Body The weight of wine in the mouth basically is the result of its extract and alcoholic content. This is the 'bone system'. Body is an important factor that varies according to the district, vintage, vinification, etc.

Tannins Although disagreeable on the palate (harsh, dry and mouth-puckering) tannins form an essential element of any young *red* wine. Tannin is extracted during fermentation from pips and skins, the thickness of the skins of red grapes and length of fermentation having a major bearing. Tannin is also derived from the wood of casks, new oak having the strongest effect. Tannins, hard and soft, are infinitely variable. Tannins precipitate proteins and act as a general preservative. Essential for long life.

Tactile stimuli Smooth, creamy, velvety qualities can be felt in the mouth; so can astringent factors, and the burning sensation of alcohol.

Flavour This is all-important. Even if it is impossible to describe, at least record whether agreeable. The word 'typical' should be used sparingly. The intensity and length of flavour reflect quality.

Balance This is basically what the wine-maker, the merchant and the connoisseur seek. What is meant by balance is that all the components are in harmony with, for example, no excess of acids or tannins at the time when the wine is ready for drinking. The point is that, individually, the components are useless, indeed mainly unpleasant to the taster; it is in combination that they become wine, and, when complete and in perfect balance, *fine* wine. Two things have to be borne in mind: one is that the intrinsic components will vary from district to district, from style to style; and that over a period of time in cask, then bottle, the balance will subtly change.

Take a red bordeaux: when young, its tannin and acidity will be exposed and raw. It takes time, say 5 to 10 years, for the components of a fine wine to simmer down and marry, becoming a well-knit harmonious drink. (It is the job of the merchant to be able to judge the future development of what, to the layman, is merely a raw young red wine.)

In the case of a fine German wine, the grower strives to achieve, almost from the start, a desirable balance of acidity, residual sugar and alcohol so that it can be early-bottled to capture, for his particular market, the delectable fruity-acidity which, with fragrant aroma and bouquet, are the touchstones of fine hocks and mosels.

Finish A clean, crisp finish is the mark of a good, well-made wine. Poor-quality wines finish short or tail off to a watery, insubstantial end.

Persistence Top-quality wines have a measurable length of taste, often extending to an aftertaste or lingering farewell – a beautiful flavour that remains in the mouth after the wine has been swallowed. The French refer to it as persistence, and measure it with a stopwatch!

Quality, finesse, elegance, breed The elements of quality are represented by the completeness and balance of the various components. Quality can be assessed by the length of time the flavour lingers in the mouth, by its richness and subtlety and by its aftertaste. A variety of expressive abstract terms can be used to express degrees of quality. They tend to be subjective and should be chosen with care. See Chapters VIII and XII.

Stage 4:

CONCLUSIONS

It should hardly be surprising that there is a relationship between the appearance, bouquet and taste of any one wine. Yet, in my experience, even competent tasters tend to examine each stage in isolation whereas some, myself included, see each stage as a revelation leading naturally to the next, and irrevocably to a logical conclusion.

Notes In practice, the experienced taster need not note precisely, in thoughts or words, his reactions to appearance, bouquet and taste; indeed, with our wonderful built-in computers, a look, a sniff and a mouthful can – if we are correctly programmed – give us instant summaries equivalent to 'a magnificent, soft, supple wine of great breed, intensity; fully mature' or 'raw, harsh, immature and poor quality – not worth buying, or keeping'.

For the student, for the beginner or for the conscientious connoisseur, a detailed tasting note arriving at a considered conclusion is a useful exercise. It gathers the thoughts and ties up the loose ends.

The conclusion, therefore, should summarize compactly the

salient points and add comments regarding the overall quality of the wine, its maturity, possibly its value and certainly its rating in the context of the tasting. *See* Chapter VII on how to make intelligible notes.

Scoring If you happen to be a judge in a competition, then almost certainly your notes and conclusions will have to be made in a precise form, usually tabulated with numerical values. Scoring is dealt with briefly on p. 73, but for exhaustive details I must refer readers to Amerine or Vedel (*see* Appendix).

Descriptions Lastly, I would again draw attention to Chapter VIII on the use of words and Chapter XII for the glossary of tasting terms. These give a wide range of commonly, and less frequently, used terms, and the definitions – which admittedly are on occasion subject to slightly different interpretations – strive to give readers not only a clear indication of their meaning but, in the case of terms like 'tannin', explain something of the physical or chemical background.

PRICE

Although not a tasting quality, price is a factor that cannot often be ignored. It is certainly the common denominator of all wine trade tastings except those concerned solely with the wine's physical development or condition.

Only a real wine snob or hypocrite (often the same person) and perhaps the carelessly rich, need not heed the price factor, though this does not mean that 'pure' or abstract tastings, comparing one wine with another, are not desirable and valuable. But for most purchasers and consumers of wine, price *is* the final arbiter, in the sense that value for money is sought and appreciated, as much as, if not more than, pure quality.

Recent years have witnessed an escalation of fine wine prices that appeared to be out of all proportion. For a time, there was a simple supply-and-demand situation – surging world demand for wines in geographically limited supply. Unhappily the speculator added pressure to the naturally increasing demands of opulent civilizations cultivating more and more wine enthusiasts. There is one consolation: the previously often impoverished wine grower at last received a return on capital, using this new-found wealth to replant derelict vineyards, replace old vines and renew equipment.

Increased production, the flight of the speculator – dumping stocks en route – and a recession then combined to reverse the market situation in the mid 1970s. For a while the price of wine dropped to levels which made sense to the drinker but which were unfortunately painful to the producer and the trade. One of the main culprits of rising prices was inflation, forcing increases in the cost of production and distribution. We really need to achieve a healthy balance between consumer, merchant and producer. If an appreciative consumer is prepared to pay a respectable merchant or restaurateur a reasonable price, this will in turn yield the vineyard owner and wine-maker a fair return for their labours, the risks and vicissitudes.

It should be remembered, however, that, historically, the finest wines have never been cheap. They were originally the sole province of the aristocratic, wealthy and privileged classes, and I dare say that quite a few did not really appreciate them to the full – then as now!

At least, by increasing our awareness and appreciation we will not waste the opportunities of tasting fine and rare wines when, as they surely will, they present themselves for our delectation.

HOW TO ORGANIZE
A TASTING

*The only way to appreciate wine is when a few men, who
understand and enjoy it meet together, feeling free to luxuriate in
the delight imparted. . . .*
T. G. Shaw
Wine, the Vine and the Cellar, 1863

Experienced wine shippers and merchants know perfectly well
how to run their own tastings. The aim of this chapter is to
advise younger members of the wine trade, amateur wine
societies and tasting groups, what preparations are necessary
and what pitfalls to avoid.

It is assumed that the purpose of a tasting is to present a range of
wines in the most favourable light either to induce sales, or
simply to learn more about wine.

The first thing is to decide what type of tasting it is to be, what
and how many wines are to be shown, and how many people
are to participate. Very often, consideration of the latter point
will dictate the number of wines and almost certainly the type
of tasting, so this factor will be dealt with first.

How many tasters?

Generally speaking, the seriousness and the effectiveness of a
tasting is inversely proportional to the number who attend. A
large propaganda tasting, attended by anything from 60 to 300
people, will require a large hall or cellar, a large staff and very
careful organization. The consumption, *per capita*, is bound to
be greater than at a small tasting; and even if, as is wise, the range
of wines is strictly limited, the expense may be out of all
proportion to the ultimate benefit.

Forty to 70 guests may be considered the maximum manage-
able number at a standard stand-up and free-roaming tasting;
rather fewer if a lecture-tasting or tutorial is envisaged.

The aim of the tasting

If the tasting is planned to launch a new branded wine, it ought
really to be limited to this alone. Rather like the press review of
a new model at the British Motor Show, the aim will be to
demonstrate the wine's desirable selling points, its drinkability,
its price, the weight of supporting advertising and the
attractions of the point-of-sale material. The gathering will
generally be confined to salesmen, their customers and members of the press, who will be expected to extol the product's
virtues. This is hardly a tasting in the wine lover's sense, but is
not infrequent in these days of sophisticated wine marketing.

More traditional are the tastings organized by the wine
importer or merchant for customers, presenting a range of
wines of a new vintage or current seasonal stock-in-trade. These
are vital and informative tastings, that benefit both trade and
consumer alike. Their proper organization is essential and the
principles involved are discussed below.

Wine society or informal group tastings, usually aimed at the
education and enlightenment of the members, who share the
cost, can be similar in style to trade tastings, and most of the
same problems arise.

But if the object is to *learn* something about wine, then by far the best type of tasting is the controlled and seated variety in the form of a lecture, with carefully selected wines used as illustrations. An event of this type will stand or fall on the knowledge and ability of the lecturer, and is probably best handled by a professional. The financial virtue of this type of tasting is that it is the most economical in terms of the amount of wine consumed.

How many wines?

At a big trade tasting there may well be from 30 to over 100 different wines on show. It goes without saying that when there is a vast number of samples, the host expects his guests to discriminate, and also to spit out. After all, trade buyers will only be in the market for wines of a certain type and price, and will not waste time, and cloud their minds, by tasting wines right out of the range of their requirements.

The minute the public is let in, however, discrimination can go by the board. Whereas the wiser and more experienced lay-tasters will concentrate on those wines that interest them most, others will treat the whole thing as a sort of cocktail party and try to drink round the room – in the long run, wasting their time and the wine merchant's money.

It is far wiser for the organizers to be selective and to show only a limited range of say 10 to 20 wines as outstanding representatives of their type and price (even fewer if they are fortified wines, i.e. port, sherry, etc.). However, if the types are mixed, do make sure they are grouped clearly and that they are tasted in the right order, heavy and sweet wines last.

Horizontal and vertical tastings

For a small club tasting or a lecture-tasting, six to 10 different wines will usually be enough. They must be well chosen, however, and worthy of study in depth. The most useful are horizontal and vertical tastings. Horizontal tastings are wines from different châteaux or different districts but all of the same vintage; vertical tastings compare different vintages of the same wine, i.e. of the same château, or of the same type or district. I have successfully combined a horizontal and vertical tasting on several occasions, with the same vintage of six different châteaux and six different vintages of one of those châteaux. The point of all this is not to make the tasting impossibly complicated but, through the comparisons, to learn more.

How much wine?

For drinking one allows approximately six to eight glasses per bottle, depending on the size of the glasses. For tasting, the number of glasses per bottle doubles, even trebles.

Allowing 12 to 15 tasting measures per bottle, the next thing is to estimate the number of glasses to be provided per person. At a controlled lecture-tasting the answer is quite simple, one per person. At a *serious* tasting where there is a big range of wines on show one can plan for a fairly small consumption on the basis that most tasters will try and taste a little of most of the wines, but one should allow extra for the more popular types of wine and provide adequate supporting stock.

However large or small the range of wines on show, one thing can be banked on: the bigger the crowd, the more will be consumed *per capita*. The hour of the day and duration of the tasting will also have a bearing.

Summing up: with a large range of wines and a small number of tasters, allow one bottle to eight or nine people; for a small range and large crowd, one bottle may serve only three or four. If it is just a casual tasting party, allow at least half-a-bottle a head. But with a smallish number at a tutored tasting, one bottle will serve 15 or more tasters.

What time of day?

The organizer has to bear in mind not only the appropriate times to taste, from the freshness of palate point of view, but the convenience of the guests. Indeed, the latter is usually of paramount importance. There are, in fact, just two practical alternatives: before lunch or early evening.*

Duration

The timing of an evening function will depend a great deal upon social conventions. The main thing to remember when planning the programme is to leave ample time for the tasting. Twenty minutes or half-an-hour is simply not enough. Half-an-hour may be sufficient if the tasting merely consists of a glass of something prior to a meal, for it then merely comes into the '7 for 7.30' category of invitation.

The length of time allowed for the tasting must be proportional to the number of wines on show and the number of guests invited. For 10 to 20 wines and 30 to 50 people the time allowed should be somewhere between one-and-a-half and two hours. The point is, that although one solid hour of tasting is more than enough for even the hardiest taster, sufficient allowance has to be made for late-comers, early leavers and social chitchat.

A controlled lecture-tasting is probably best held in the evening. The length of time required will depend partly upon the speaker. Two hours just sitting, sipping and listening is the absolute maximum. On the other hand, it is surprising how long it can take to taste and talk about only half-a-dozen wines. One should aim at about one-and-a-quarter to one-and-a-half hours. Incidentally, it is most important that everyone arrives on time, so invitations should be explicit: 7 for 7.15 prompt, or words to this effect.

Big trade tastings are usually organized in suitable premises (in firms' cellars, even in the town hall) by experienced professionals, so we will confine our attentions to two moderate-sized types of tasting.

A FREE-RANGING TASTING FOR *20 to 60* GUESTS

Space and flow

Ideally, the organizer removes everything that will interfere with table layout and customer-flow. At all costs clutter must be avoided; there will be little enough room for assistants and impedimenta. Crowds bring their own problems and one of the first, too often overlooked, is hats, coats and bags. If there is not a cloakroom or spare room nearby, then set aside a large table for coats, etc.

---

*I used to think that serious tastings could not take place during a meal, but I have been privileged to attend a quite remarkable series of dinner tastings. The earliest were organized by Joseph Berkmann, then one of London's most enterprising restaurateurs. It surprised me how effective as well as interesting tasting a large range at table could be.

The most important considerations after this are spatial: there must be enough room for tasters to circulate without obstruction; there must be enough space between the different wines to allow tasters adequate elbow room; and also enough space, preferably barred to tasters, for staff and assistants to service the tasting tables.

Table layout

The key to success is table layout. This will depend on the shape of the room, but basically there are two approaches: to have a series of tables round the room (continuous or spaced) with the tasters circulating in the middle, or to have a 'square' of tables in the centre, enclosing staff and stock. The virtues of the latter are that fewer assistants are needed to supervise the tasting – opening bottles, keeping them in order, removing empty bottles and used glasses – and that the service and stock areas are safely isolated (but bear in mind that assistants have to push through tasters to get to the central reservation).

If a large number of wines are on display it is probably better to arrange the tables around the perimeter of the room; they can be spaced better, and tasters can move from one area to another more easily. Avoid corners, however, as these can become congested.

Staff must be stationed at *each* table section, so at a big tasting this will mean one assistant per two- or three-metre section or per six wines.

Space requirements are often underestimated, particularly the space between different wines. Apart from the discomfort caused by nudgers, wines get mixed up and out of order if set out too closely. To avoid this, allow only four to six bottles to a three-metre trestle table, depending on the number of tasters expected. The more tasters, the wider the spacing.

Sequence

The wines should be laid out in the correct order of tasting and, most important but not always easy, incoming guests must be made aware of the sequence of wines and encouraged to taste in that order. This is where a clearly laid-out tasting sheet comes in handy: list order and table layout should coincide. One very important point: do not place table number one too near the entrance as a queue of early tasters may form and impede the passage of other guests and assistants.

If the room is small it is usually better to start the tasting on the far side to avoid congestion. If there are sweet or fortified wines in a mixed tasting, place them at the end of the natural tasting sequence and traffic flow to discourage guests from tasting them first.

Side tables

Still on the subject of layout, and ignoring for the moment decoration and other incidentals, it is better to have quite separate tables for glasses, food and literature. Ideally, the table for glasses and tasting sheets should be placed somewhere between the entrance and the first wine to be tasted. Informative literature of the take-home variety should be handed out from a table by the exit. No purpose is served by burdening guests with supplementary reading matter at the start or part-way through the tasting: there is seldom time to read it during the tasting and the odds are that it will be discarded before the tasting is over.

Placing of spittoons

Spittoons are not easy to place. They should not be on the tasting tables but on the floor, either just in front of the tables (if the wines are well spaced and there is ample room for tasters' feet) *or* sufficiently away from the tables not to trip people up. They are probably best placed two or three metres from the tables, more if large crowds are expected, to allow an appropriate width of passage for circulation and to encourage tasters to retreat from the table with their tasting samples, permitting other tasters a chance to get to the tables. There is nothing more irritating at a tasting than clinging vines who station themselves semipermanently by a bottle, helping themselves, making notes and spitting, all without moving their feet. Out-of-reach spittoons help to dislodge the blockers.

A 'TUTORED' TASTING

The room size required must be directly related to the numbers attending: each taster, as well as the lecturer, will need a chair and table space.

Tables essential

Make no mistake about it, tables are vital. It is impossible to conduct this sort of tasting session with tasting sheets, pencils, glasses and possibly maps and other literature on one's lap.

Either individual small tables or desks should be used, allocating one per taster. Larger tables may, of course, be shared. In any case, the spacing per person must be wider than a chair's width. Allow at least a metre per taster so that there is room on each section of table for several glasses in a row, and the tasting sheet.

It is much more comfortable for all tasters to face the lecturer, so only one side of the table should be used. If the tables are in continuous rows then there must be sufficient space between those rows for the assistants to pour or hand out glasses. It is a mistake to assume that fewer helpers are required for lecture-tastings, for although there may be just one lecturer, the timing of the service of the wines is very important and sufficient serving staff or willing volunteers must be available.

Wine service

There are two ways of serving the wine: either pouring into glasses already on the table, or pre-pouring and handing out glasses. I favour the latter. Assuming that a tasting quantity will range from about 10 to 15 glasses per bottle, it is desirable to have one assistant per bottle, i.e. per 10 to 15 tasters, otherwise the time taken pouring is apt to disturb the lecturer and fragment the session. It is difficult for tasters to concentrate whilst assistants are moving around with the wine, and if the service is protracted there is always the danger that those who get the wine first will be tempted to taste the wine 'solo' instead of waiting to be guided through the elements of colour, bouquet and taste by the lecturer. Frankly, I think the quickest and fairest way is to pour careful measures into glasses on trays in an adjacent room and hand them out at precisely the moment they are called for by the lecturer.

The problem of spittoons is even more acute with a seated audience. They should be behind the chairs, one between two tasters being ideal. Alternatively, small plastic cups can be placed on the table before each taster. But with a restricted number of wines no harm is done if the wine is swallowed.

DETAILS TO BEAR IN MIND

────────────────── **Tables** ──────────────────

It may seem silly to say this, but the essential thing is that tables should be of normal dinner-table height, and firm. In other words, do not use tiny coffee tables or flimsy, unstable trestle tables. Nor should the tables used be too high or too wide, as it can be awkward to serve across them.

────────────── **Table coverings** ──────────────

There are several factors to consider: red wine stains; bottles can scratch; and a white background is essential to show off the colour of the wine. So, cover the table, whether it is plain deal or polished mahogany. If the latter, use a large white cloth with newspaper or some other lining underneath. If an ordinary trestle table is used, a white table cloth or rolls of plain white paper can be pinned to it.

────────────────── **Lighting** ──────────────────

This is important, and yet often the least-considered factor. A natural north light is best; failing that, tungsten or warm-white fluorescent lighting. Ordinary blue fluorescent lighting is disastrous. It gives red wine an unhealthy dark, blue-black tinge and will make it appear far younger and less mature than it really is. Candles add appropriate glamour to the occasion but, truthfully, although a myriad of candles may look pretty, they really do not produce enough of the sort of light in which the colour of the wine can be effectively judged. Mind you, there is no reason why candles, either in proper candelabra or stuck in the top of empty bottles, should not be used in conjunction with artificial light. One or two per table look attractive, and they are useful for observing the clarity of the wine. But do remember: candles consume oxygen and add to the heat of the room.

────────────── **Service or self-service?** ──────────────

At an ordinary, largish tasting, is it better for the hosts to pour out the wine, or should guests be allowed to help themselves? In practice, whatever is decided, there is usually a bit of both. At a well-attended tasting, the staff will be busy doing several jobs at once and it is fairly certain that they will not be able to spend all their time helping the guests to wine, even if this is supposed to be their main job.

On the other hand, if tasters help themselves too liberally at a free-for-all tasting, then a bit of judicious and tactful pouring will be called for. This will prevent the host's stocks being depleted too rapidly and will encourage guests to taste a wider range more effectively.

────────────── **Assistants and staff** ──────────────

Do not underestimate the number of people required to help, from supervisor to cloakroom attendant. Numbers and calibre of staff will, of course, depend on the nature of the event, its size and the place.

Small club tastings are usually no problem. Just make sure there are members prepared to lend a hand. Many small- and medium-sized trade tastings are manned by members of the firm, usually principals and sales staff who know their subject and are identifiable by lapel badges bearing their name and/or that of their company.

When tastings are held in catering establishments – hotels, restaurants or clubs – staff will generally be employed. Even if supervised by a head waiter or captain, it should never be assumed that they will know exactly what is required. So a cardinal rule is to *brief all staff before the tasting commences*: where to station themselves, how many bottles to open, how much to pour; to clear glasses and avoid clutter, etc.

Insist on rigorous stock control, with a complete complement of bottles, full or empty, after the tasting, otherwise bottles simply disappear. Another tip is to provide a supply of inexpensive wine or beer for the staff to refresh themselves – preferably afterwards.

Let *one* person be in overall charge. Have enough 'front of house' personnel to host and advise; enough staff or assistants to serve. Do not forget to man the cloakroom and reception table. Make sure everyone knows precisely what he or she is to do.

Spittoons, bottles and funnels

Properly equipped tasting rooms have permanent spittoons of a basin, fountain or flushing variety. At the sort of tastings we have just been discussing, however, mobile spittoons are the order of the day and they run to three types: the pedestal-funnel variety, rather like a fat version of one of the nastier types of road-house ash-tray; the sawdust box or bucket; and the table-top bowl or cup.

Quite the simplest to prepare and satisfactory to use is the sawdust box. This type of spittoon is just a wooden wine case with the top removed and the inside two-thirds filled with sawdust. It is commodious and fairly absorbent; to be on the safe side, line it with oil-cloth or polythene. The disadvantage is that it is easy to trip over a box in a crowded room.

If you cannot find enough boxes, buckets of sand or sawdust will do. They present a smaller target, however, and knock over more easily. Never use glass tumblers as table-top spittoons: wine spittal looks horrible. Polystyrene or opaque plastic cups are best. Incidentally, empty bottles, with glass or plastic funnels stuck in the neck, seen on tables at many trade tastings, are *not* spittoons. They are receptacles for the taster to empty his glass in before moving to the next wine. Take care that they do not overflow: magnums are most suitable for this purpose. One often wonders about what happens to all the secondhand but almost virginal wine which is accumulated (staff perks? cooking wine? or re-corked as Château Grand-Mélange?).

Glasses

Clear, tulip-shaped, stemmed glasses are desirable. Naturally, at a large tasting, quantity and not quality of glassware must prevail. Standard goblets are perfectly adequate and can be hired at a reasonable price from any reputable catering firm. The 6-oz (170-ml) size tends to be too big for a tasting; 5-oz (140-ml) glasses are more economical, or even, at a pinch, large port glasses. Other suitable types are sherry *copitas* and 'dock' glasses. The ideal tasting glass is illustrated on p. 49.

The quantity of glasses required needs careful consideration. All depends on the number of different wines on show and people expected. Except at a seated tasting, it is rarely a practical proposition to provide one glass per person per wine. At a large tasting one glass is normally provided on arrival and the taster is expected to use it throughout the tasting, though a clean glass is usually obtainable if by chance the first is abandoned or if a fresh one is really required. If wines of contrasting colour and style are shown at the same tasting a change of glasses should be allowed for. Even if the basis is one glass per taster, allowance must be made for wastage: breakages, abandoned glasses, etc., so order double the number first thought of.

Nothing looks worse than a litter of partially filled glasses, particularly on tasting tables, so staff should continually remove them. If they are left on the tables they just get in the way and encourage other people to abandon theirs too.

If there are insufficient glasses, or if proper washing-up facilities are not available, it may be necessary to put rinsing bowls in the tasting room. They tend to look unsightly, however, and might be objected to on the grounds of hygiene. If assistants are expected to wash glasses on the spot, washing-up bowls should be either behind the table out of sight or on a rear service table.

How many bottles?

Even at a big and busy tasting it is better to have only *one* bottle of each wine open at a time. This is not just for the sake of economy; its main purpose is to avoid clutter and to prevent the bottles from getting out of order. It also discourages guests from picking up open bottles and wandering off with them, ostensibly to assist their friends. It usually stays with the group until it is consumed!

Nor should the entire tasting stock of bottles of each wine be put on the table in serried ranks. They may look impressive, but they soon get in the way of the serving staff. Bottles are picked up for a close look at the label – and usually put back in the wrong place, all of which adds to the disorganization and mess. However, it is not a bad idea to have one other bottle, opened but stoppered, alongside the tasting bottle. It acts as an immediate reserve and enables waiting tasters to look at the label and the general presentation of the bottle. The point is, it is difficult to see the label of a wine being poured; it is usually obscured by hand or napkin. Last, but not least, the number of wines open for tasting may be dictated by the heat of the room. A cold white wine can gain 10°F (5°C) in as many minutes.*

Corks and capsules

The presentation of sample bottles is important. The capsules should be cut as for a dinner party, just below the top of the neck and the top removed. Do not remove the entire capsule. Next wipe the top of neck and cork with a damp cloth and finally with a clean dry cloth.

After removing the cork, preferably in one piece – not so easy with older wines – it should be tied to the neck, wine-side up, with a rubber band. Lastly a wedge-shaped stopper cork is inserted until it is time to serve.

Older red wines should, of course, be decanted. Make sure the decanter is identified by name or number. The empty bottle is then placed alongside, with cork, for inspection.

Food?

Except at press receptions and the more social type of tasting, food should be kept to a minimum. It merely distracts and

*An ideal solution is the use of Vinicool® transparent plastic open-topped vacuum flasks. *See* p. 130

provides counter-flavours and smells. Nevertheless, it must be accepted that some people need something to cleanse their palates between wines. Cheese squares and dry biscuits are the conventional answer to this problem; dry bread and plain cold water are alternatives. (Iced water stuns the palate.)

It is perhaps important also to bear in mind that virtually all red wines and most whites have been devised by nature and man as an accompaniment for food. In fact, wine tastes different with food and, if it is to be judged in a food context, it is often easier to do so at a tasting with an appropriate nibble.

The old saying 'buy a wine over apples and sell it over cheese' has much more than a grain of truth in it. Cheese makes wine taste softer, mellower and sweeter. The riper and more 'smelly' cheeses are all right with rougher reds, but they tend to overpower delicate wines. An overripe brie will kill a mature burgundy stone dead. The other problems with richer and more exotic cheeses are that their smell will compete with the bouquet of the wine.

So small squares of a mild cheese of the cheddar variety are safe and satisfactory: one generous plateful per tasting table.

Reverting to apples for a moment, one English wine merchant, renowned for his port, used to clean his palate with a bite of apple between tasting samples of young vintage port. A noted taster in Oporto consumes charcoal before his morning tasting of young ports. I confess I have not tried these though sorely tempted. There are few wines more palate-numbing than immature port.

No smoking – or strong scent

One would have thought that the 'no smoking' rule at tastings was sufficiently known and understood. But it seems that smokers are a law unto themselves; they do not even consider the spent matches and cigarette ends as litter, but unthinkingly discard them anywhere. A man who reaches automatically for his pipe and pouch at home will do so with equal unconcern when he has reached the contemplative end of a tasting.

So, beware. At a big public tasting put NO SMOKING signs up. Catch smokers politely at the door and advise all assistants to watch out for the telltale wreaths of blue smoke, particularly among the groups who are chatting in a relaxed fashion, their tasting completed.

Everyone attending a tasting should also refrain from using strong scent, powder, aftershave lotion, etc. The delicate bouquet of wine simply cannot compete with a host of foreign smells; it is difficult enough as it is without one's nostrils being assaulted by smoke and perfume at the same time.

Tasting sheets

There is no surer way of wasting one's efforts than to invite guests to taste without providing some form of score-card – a printed list, folder or tasting sheet – for them to consult, make comments on, and take away afterwards.

There are three essential requirements:

● The sheet should contain the full name and vintage of each wine listed in tasting order, with prices if a trade tasting.

● There should be space for comments either alongside or underneath each wine, or on a blank page opposite. At least as much space should be allowed for notes as the name of the wine occupies.

● It should be printed on card or stiff paper. Flimsy paper is hopeless. Alternatively, provide clipboards.

Embellishments such as wine maps and descriptions of wine districts, etc. can be included. Occasionally price list and tasting sheet are combined. The scope for variety is immense; but whatever form it takes, a tasting sheet is basically an *aide-mémoire*; for with wine, as with many other things, it is a matter of 'in at one ear and out of the other'.

Licensing laws

Before concluding this chapter, a few words on licensing laws are in order. This section, of necessity, must confine itself to the British Isles, the licensing laws of which are complex enough without having to go further afield. Curiously, English licensing laws are surprisingly inexplicit on the subject of tastings.

The moment money changes hands or licensed premises are used for tastings, the laws of the land must be observed.

First, it is illegal for *any* person in an unlicensed situation (in the sense that, although there are licence-*holders*, it is *premises* that are licensed to sell wines, etc.) to sell wine by the bottle or glass. Strictly speaking, you cannot sell a bottle from your own private cellar to a friend without breaking the law. Bottles can only be sold from licensed premises, either fully licensed or 'off'-licensed. If an off-licence only is held, it is illegal for customers to pay for tasting samples, either by way of an entrance fee or per glass or per bottle if those samples are tasted on the premises.★ Most wine merchants are in this position, but there is nothing wrong in their offering free samples for tasting, except in Scotland, where this is regarded, not illogically, as an inducement to make an eventual sale.

Only in 'on'-licensed premises (public houses, hotels and such-like – 'table' licences excluded) can tasting samples be sold by glass or bottle for consumption (which includes tasting and spitting out) there and then.

Tasters under the age of 18 are not permitted to consume wine on licensed premises, but there are no restrictions elsewhere.

Unlicensed amateurs are not so circumscribed. They can happily organize tastings at home, or in any other unlicensed premises. What they must remember, however, is not to *sell* wine to each other or to non-members of a tasting group – even for charity. The organizers of big charity tastings might be advised to clear their position beforehand with the police, H.M. Customs and Excise or local magistrate's court.

A wine merchant or his representative can also hold a tasting of his stock-in-trade on unlicensed premises, so long as he makes no charge for entry or sale by the glass. He can also solicit orders at such a tasting so long as the orders are effected, i.e. the wines delivered, from off-licensed premises.

To the organizers of private tastings my advice is, if in doubt say nothing; get on with it. A cautious official, not quite sure of laws of the land, may play safe at your expense. But if money changes hands, beware.

Summary

Plan the tasting well in advance. Consider all the vital factors: date, time, place; number of guests and assistants; the type and number of wines. Do not leave important details until the last minute. The check list opposite may come in handy.

★Though I understand that a *bona-fide* tasting club can charge for these events.

CHECK LIST FOR TASTINGS

In advance

Guest list
Room booking
Wine selection and stock reservation
Printing: invitations, tasting sheets
Order tables, cloths, glasses and other accessories
Forewarn assistants; book staff

Pretasting checks

Cloakroom facilities
Tasting room layout
Tables: number, size, arrangement
Table cloths or rolls of white paper
Wine (preferably delivered in advance, to settle); temperature of wine and of room
Two bottles of each wine at each tasting position; supporting stock handy but not on view
Corkscrews: one per assistant or one per table (there are never enough)
Stopper corks, wedge-shaped
Rubber bands for securing original corks to bottle necks
Lapel badges for hosts and assistants
Glasses: right quantity, shape and size (polished *and* clean-smelling)
Lighting: correct intensity, type and position
Spittoons, sawdust boxes or plastic cups
Cloths or napkins for glasses and wiping bottle necks (one per assistant)
Empty bottles (magnums) with funnels for dregs
Candles, candelabra or empty bottles, and matches
Rinsing bowls, if necessary
Plain cheese cubes, and plates
Dry biscuits or dry bread, and plates
Jugs of water (without ice)
Trays for removal of glasses
Tasting sheets
Price lists, supporting literature, hand-outs, press kits
Sharpened pencils or ball-point pens
Maps, posters, drawing pins and adhesive tape
Visitors' book
NO SMOKING signs (remove ash trays to discourage smokers)
Lock-up room for storage of wine, particularly on strange premises

Staff, assistants

Brief all staff carefully before tasting commences
Allocate stands, tables, duties
Number of bottles to be opened, timing
Keep tables uncluttered, remove empty glasses
Boozers, free-loaders and smokers – refer to organizer

After the tasting

Separation of unopened, opened and empty bottles
Stock check

VII

HOW TO RECORD TASTING NOTES

. . . add a little to the literature of one of the three great joys in life.
George Saintsbury
Notes on a Cellar-book

Only two kinds of person can do without tasting notes: the rare and fortunate individual with a phenomenally freak memory, and the less rare type who chooses not to complicate matters by ever tasting more than the firm favourites he knows and likes. (There is, in fact, a third: the really experienced specialist who spends every day tasting wines in his own particular field. For example, the sherry, port or whisky blender. His highly developed palate for a comparatively limited range of smells and tastes may not require the support of the written word, save to record the names and proportions of the constituent parts selected for the blend.)

So, make notes. They will be useful, and referring back to them enjoyable.

Essential information

Frankly, any system is adequate that stores sufficient information for an individual's purpose in a speedy and accessible manner.

The following information is more or less essential:
- The date of tasting (too often omitted in the heat of the moment)
- The name of the wine (district, vineyard)
- The vintage year
- If in bottle, the name of the bottler (if estate-bottled the name of the estate. Château-bottlings merely require the qualifying initials C.B.). If from the cask, 'ex cask'
- The price (per bottle, per dozen or per cask or *tonneau*, as appropriate)
- A description of the appearance of the wine: depth, colour, clarity
- A description of its nose: aroma, bouquet
- A description of its taste: components, length, finish
- General conclusions: maturity, quality, value.

One important point should be made. Just because there are myriads of descriptive terms available it is not essential or desirable to overdo it; indeed, the experienced taster will tend to note only the outstanding and most meaningful characteristics, the faults and the exceptions.

A typical page of entries from my own tasting notebooks is given on p. 98. I note the occasion, the host, the place and, if it is a special dinner, the food. I also index each wine by country and district, but frankly these details are up to the individual.

Card system

Of the various methods of collating tasting notes the card system has many virtues. A separate card for each wine is stored in district, vintage or alphabetical order. This system is very handy for quick reference. Appropriate sections can be extracted and taken to the tasting room thus saving considerable time as headings are already prepared. The main disadvantages are that it is a bulky system and individual cards can get misplaced.

────────────── **Tasting book** ──────────────

Notes are entered as the wines are tasted, in chronological order. The advantage of this system is that a series of pocket-sized books instead of boxes of cards can be used. The pages can be ruled vertically to save rewriting main headings.

The disadvantages are the amount of work required (details of each wine have to be entered every time) and the need for an accurate and up-to-date index for quick reference. Neverthe-less, this is the type I have always used for my tasting daybooks.

────────────── **Ring binders** ──────────────

Another system combines the virtues of card and book. It consists of ruled or printed leaves, arranged horizontally and set into a ring or spiral binder. It is used like a book but leaves can be inserted as and where necessary. This, as a matter of interest, is the sort I use for the bordeaux and port notes I extract from my daybooks and arrange in vintage order.

Like the card system, the wines can be kept in any order – district, vintage or alphabetical. (But the system tends to be bulky unless several wines can be written up on one page.)

────────────── **Analytical score cards** ──────────────

Wines submitted to a panel of judges for comparative and competitive tasting have to be tasted methodically. Almost invariably a printed tasting card is supplied, indicating the factors to be noted and assessed and giving each factor, or each group, a numerical value.

Points are awarded for positive features; negative points for faults. Maximum possible can be 7 points, more often 20, sometimes 100.

The points weighting depends on the type and class of wine to be tasted, and the purpose of the tasting. For commercial entries judges might be allowed up to 4 points for colour, 6 for bouquet and 10 for taste; possibly 5, 5 and 10.

There are a variety of highly sophisticated and elaborate score cards used for equally varied types of tasting. But the vast majority are employed for either assessing and evaluating fairly closely related commercial wines, either at the academic level, producer or big trade buying levels, or at the various competitions which take place regularly in wine-producing countries: for example in Mâcon, France, Orange County, California, and in the wine states of Australia. In addition, meticulous tastings along fairly rigid lines are conducted by professionals in their own regions, for example in the major German wine areas to award seals of quality.

When dealing with wines of a similar type, perhaps lacking the marked varietal characteristics, shades of colour, nose and taste of fine vintage wines, verbal descriptions tend to be inadequate and numerical ratings take their place. But just because some of these tastes and smells are so similar and hard to rate, and because all human beings are fallible – and most wine tasters impressionable – double checks are required. Hence the importance of statistical procedures, triangular tests and so forth, in strictly academic and commercial tastings. To accom-plish this, the same wines are presented blind, in very clinical conditions, in varying orders. The object of these exercises is to eliminate bias and to establish, as objectively as possible, the validity of the tastings, the taste preferences and relative suitability of wines in a given context.

It is also important to test the tasters. One taster's susceptibility to sulphur dioxide, to volatile acidity, even to sweetness will be different from another's. The level at which smells and tastes can be perceived by even experienced tasters, is not necessarily the same for tannins, the various types of acidity and sugars.

Members of professional tasting panels should be trained and those selected for competition judging must not only have proven ability but be given a clear idea of the parameters of such tastings: what to look for, what to take note of and, most important of all, on what basis points should be awarded. In Australia, for example, tasters begin as assistants to the State or area judging panel, arranging the tastings, helping out, studying the form. They then graduate to the tasting panel itself, the senior members of which eventually 'graduate' as national show judges.

─────── **Examples of numerical ratings** ───────

Systems abound, all awarding plus or minus points to facets of appearance, nose and taste. A brief summary of some of the better known follow.

The Davis Scorecard was evolved at the famous Department of Enology at the University of California, Davis, whose graduates fill many, probably most, of the major technical positions at wineries throughout that state, and further afield.

The original Davis scorecard was as follows:

appearance	2	points
color	2	,,
aroma and bouquet	4	,,
volatile acidity	2	,,
total acidity	2	,,
sweetness	1	,,
body	1	,,
flavor	2	,,
bitterness	2	,,
general quality	2	,,

A 'superior' wine would rate 17 to 20, standard 13 to 16, below standard 9 to 12, unacceptable or spoiled 1 to 8.

It will quickly be noticed that a taster, however gifted, cannot be pulled off the street and be expected to rate a wine with even a superficially simple point system such as this without an explanation of both the terms and the weighting. In fact problems arose and a modified scorecard was introduced:

appearance	2
color	2
aroma and bouquet	6
total acidity	2
sweetness	1
body	1
flavor	2
bitterness	1
astringency	1
general quality	2

An amateur would have difficulty in differentiating 'bitterness' and 'astringency'. Indeed, this sort of tasting rating is very much one for professionals who see eye to eye.

Another 20-point system roughly following the modified Davis scale seems simpler:

clarity	2
color	2
aroma	2
bouquet	2
acidity	1
balance	2
body	2
taste	3
finish	2
overall	2

Even so, each member of the panel has to have a clear idea of precisely what facet scores what. Finally, to test the significance of scores an elaborate series of statistical procedures have been devised at Davis. These are exhaustively dealt with by Amerine and Roessler (*see* Appendix).

My personal view is that these numerical scoring systems are doubtless valid and useful for the more humdrum wines but do not begin to aid the taster to form a meaningful assessment of fine wines.

The system used in Germany for their seals of quality is far more explicit. The following relates to German white wines:

1. Colour:	colourless	0
	onion skin	0
	pale	1
	typical	2
2. Clarity:	cloudy	0
	brilliant	2
3. Bouquet:	faulty	0
	mute	1
	clean	2
	fine	3
	fragrant and flavoury	4
4. Flavour:	faulty	0
	acceptable	1–3
	thin but characteristic	4–6
	balanced	7–9
	ripe and noble	10–12

The minimum points for an award are, respectively, 2, 2, 2 and 6 points; for Kabinett quality a minimum total of 13, for Auslese 15, Beerenauslese 16 and Trockenbeerenauslese 17.

The Italian National Order of Winetasters uses the Buxbaum system which has a maximum of 20 positive points for the best, and 10 for the worst, 'demerito'.

The French, as can be expected, have perhaps the most complete and sophisticated scoring systems and tasting cards. Distinguished academic tasters' names include Chabanon, Max Léglise, Emile Peynaud, Jacques Puisais, J. Ribereau-Gayon and A. Vedel.

The OIV (Office International de la Vigne et du Vin) has an ingenious and Gallically complicated scorecard which I first witnessed in use at an international wine competition in Budapest. Contrarily, the perfect score is zero, the judges noting defects which are then multiplied to arrive at the qualifying score. The card used for each wine is as follows:

Element	Weighting	Defects multiplied by				
		× 0	× 1	× 4	× 9	× 16
Appearance	1					
Colour	1					
Intensity of odour	1					
Quality of odour	2					
Intensity of taste	2					
Quality of taste	3					
Harmony/balance	2					

Outstanding features qualify for the 0 column, very good in column 1, good 4, acceptable 9 and unacceptable 16.

Once again, judges using such a score card must have explained to them precisely what is meant by the various terms and relative weightings.

Some tasters use a 10-point scale, some even 100 – though how a score such as $85\frac{1}{2}$ can be justified or remotely equalled on a subsequent occasion I do not know.

Which brings me to my final point about scoring. The only virtue, as far as I can see, of a points system is in the context of a *range* of wines on one occasion: which wine was, at that moment of time, considered best. And even then I regard a full description of each wine as more important, the total score being helpful to refer to at a later date when words fail to convey precisely which, say, of two good wines one slightly preferred at that tasting.

If ever I resort to scoring, I use a simple 20 point rating:

Appearance *(depth, colour, clarity, viscosity)*	3
Nose *(grape aroma, bouquet, condition, development)*	6
Taste *(dryness, body, tannin, acidity, flavour, length)*	6
Overall Quality *(balance, finish, complexity, finesse)*	5

For the record, Hugh Johnson and I put our heads together to devise a tasting scorecard for the Sunday Times Wine Club. It is reproduced on the opposite page.

Descriptive rating cards

A variety of purely descriptive, as opposed to numerical, tasting cards have been published, but outstandingly the most interesting, again not surprisingly, is French. Steven Spurrier has kindly given me permission to reprint his English adaptation of the card devised by Castell and published by INAO. *See* following pages. For greater detail see *Academie du Vin Wine Course* (Century Publishing in association with Christie's).

The only problem with this elaborate card is that it is bulky and perhaps, for the advanced taster, somewhat inhibits the imagination and development of one's own vocabulary.

◉ THE CHRISTIE'S – SUNDAY TIMES WINE CLUB TASTING CHART ◉

		Comments
Name of Wine District/type Merchant/bottler	Vintage Date purchased Price	
SIGHT Score (Maximum 4) ☐ CLARITY cloudy, bitty, dull, clear, brilliant DEPTH OF COLOUR watery, pale, medium, deep, dark COLOUR (White wines) green tinge, pale yellow, yellow, gold, brown (Red wines) purple, purple/red, red, red/brown VISCOSITY slight sparkle, watery, normal, heavy, oily	starbright, tuilé, straw, amber, tawny, ruby, garnet, oeil de perdrix, hazy, opaque	
SMELL Score (Maximum 4) ☐ GENERAL APPEAL neutral, clean, attractive, outstanding off (eg. yeasty, acetic, oxidized, woody, etc.) FRUIT AROMA none, slight, positive, identifiable eg. riesling BOUQUET none, pleasant, complex, powerful	cedarwood, corky, woody, dumb, flowery, smoky, honeyed, lemony, spicy, mouldy, peardrops, sulphury	
TASTE Score (Maximum 9) ☐ SWEETNESS (white wines) bone dry, dry, medium dry, medium, sweet, very sweet TANNIN (red wines) astringent, marked, dry, soft ACIDITY flat, refreshing, marked, tart BODY very light and thin, light, medium, full bodied, heavy LENGTH short, acceptable, extended, lingering BALANCE unbalanced, good, very well balanced, perfect	apple, bitter, burning, blackcurrants, caramel, dumb earthy, fat, flinty, green, heady, inky, flabby, mellow, metallic, mouldy, nutty, salty, sappy, silky, spicy, fleshy, woody, watery	
OVERALL QUALITY Score (Maximum 3) ☐ Coarse, poor, acceptable, fine, outstanding	supple, finesse, breed, elegance harmonious, rich, delicate	**HOW TO USE THIS CHART** Wine appeals to three senses: sight, smell and taste. This card is a guide to analyzing its appeal and an aide-memoire on each wine you taste. Tick one word for each factor in the left-hand column and any of the descriptive terms which fit your impressions. Then award points according to the pleasure the wine gives you. Use the right-hand column for your comments.
SCORING Total score (out of 20)	DATE OF TASTING	

Compiled by Hugh Johnson and Michael Broadbent M.W. © 1975

Wine Type (White/Rosé/Red)	
Appellation:	**Type:**
Laboratory observations and conclusion	**Date of Analysis**
Specific Gravity	Total Acidity
Alcohol	Fixed Acidity
Residual Sugar	Volatile Acidity
Potential Alcohol	(corrected for sulphuric acid)
Total SO_2 pH	
Free SO_2 colour index P/x	
Index of permanganate	

Method of Vinification

Visual Examination	

Surface of the liquid *Brilliant – dull. Clean – iridescent – oily*

Colour

White Wine	*Pale with green or yellow tints – pale yellow – straw yellow – canary yellow – gold – amber*
Rosé Wine	*Pale with violet or rose tints – grey – light rose – deep rose – partridge eye – onion skin*
Red Wine	*Red with crimson or violet tints – cherry red – ruby – garnet red – red brown – tile red – mahogany – tawny*
Hue	*Frank – oxidized – cloudy*

Aspect

Crystalline – brilliant – limpid – hazy – cloudy – turgid – lead grey/white – opaque, with or without deposit

Legs/Tears

Quick or slow to form – non-existent – slight – heavy

Temperature of the wine	**Any factor hindering the tasting**

Olfactory Examination	

First Impression *Pleasant – ordinary – unpleasant*

Aroma

Intensity	*Powerful – adequate – feeble – non-existent*
Quality	*Very fine – racy – distinguished – fine – ordinary – common – not very pleasant – unpleasant*
Character	*Primary – secondary – tertiary – floral – fruity – vegetal – spicy – animal – oxidized*
Length	*Long – average – short*

Abnormal odours

CO_2 – SO_2 – H_2S – *mercaptan – strongly oxidized – woody – lactic acid*

acescence – phenolic – corky

flaw	*temporary – permanent*
	slight – serious

Details

Any factor hindering or stopping the continuation of the tasting

Gustatory Examination	
First Impression	
Flavours and sensations	
Sweetness	
Sugar	*Heavy – very sweet – sweet – dry – brut*
Glycerine and alcohol	*Soft – unctuous – velvety – smooth – rough – dried out*
Acidity	
Excessive	*Acid – green – tart – nervy – acidulous*
Balanced	*Fresh – lively – supple – smooth*
Insufficient	*Flat – flabby*
Body	
Alcoholic strength	*Light – sufficient – generous – heady – hot*
Flesh	*Fat – round – full – thin – meagre*
Tannin	*Rich – balanced – insufficient – astringent – bitter*
Aromas in the mouth	
Intensity	*Powerful – average – weak – long – short*
Quality	*Very fine – elegant – pleasant – common – faded*
Nature	*Floral – fruity – vegetable – spicy – wood – chemical – animal – other* *young – developed – complex*
Inherent or Abnormal Flavours	
'Terroir'	*Marked – noticeable – faint – non-existent*
Sickness	*Grease – turned – aldehydes – sweet – sour – rancid – acetic acid – lactic acid*
Accident	*Stagnant – mould – lees – woody – cork – metallic – H_2S – herbaceous – acrid*
Final Impression	
Balance	*Harmonious – bold – correct – unbalanced* *Xs acid, Xs sugar, Xs tannin, Xs alcohol*
After taste	*Straightforward – unpleasant*
Resistance of taste and aroma	*> 8 sec 5–7 sec 4–5 sec < 3 sec* *Very long – long – medium – short*
Conclusions	
Conformity to appellation or type	
Score out of 20	
Summary of tasting (character of wine – future, readiness for drinking)	

──────────────── **Ratings and medals** ────────────────

Most professionals are wary of medals awarded at wine competitions, and, every so often, the organizers of such competitions have something of a purge, determining to give medals sparingly to avoid their devaluation and subsequent loss of credibility resulting from overmarketing.

By and large, competitions are organized in wine producing areas and open mainly to wine from those areas.

In Australia, where annual wine competitions not only thrive but are taken very seriously by the producers, high awards can lead to big sales. There, to qualify for a gold medal a wine has to score 18.5 or more out of 20; for a silver 17 to 18.4, and for a bronze 15.5 to 16.9. California has a number of similar events.

In France the highest award is generally the *Grande Médaille d'Or*, next comes the *Médaille d'Or*, then *Médaille d'Argent* followed by *2me Diplôme d'Honneur* and *3me Diplôme d'Honneur*. England has only one competition for local wine producers, awarding Gold, Silver and Bronze medals. The outright winner is presented with the Gore-Browne Trophy, donated by a redoubtable lady wine-growing pioneer in memory of her husband. However, not to be outdone, England also boasts an international wine competition, the brain-child of Anton Massel and his Oenological Research Laboratory, in which wines of different types and origins are judged in their respective classes. Medals are awarded annually, 'double-golds' being not uncommon.

There is no doubt that competition is healthy, and if the possibility of winning a medal will induce wine producers to strive for even better quality, so much the better for the eventual consumer.

Another benefit is the opportunity to compare; to see what one's rivals are up to and with what success. If the judges are fair and representative, the producer can perhaps gain a clearer idea of what style of wine has the greatest appeal. And of course the attendant publicity is good.

The one major snag is that some really top class wineries, such as Heitz in California, care not to enter their wine. They have an established reputation which does not need the endorsement of a medal. For Château Lafite or the Domaine de la Romanée-Conti, entering such competitions would be demeaning and any subsequent award superfluous. And there is always the nagging worry that they might not come top!

COLOUR VARIATIONS

The appearance of wine can be most meaningful. Fill a generous tasting glass to about a third full with a good wine. Observe the depth of colour at a 45° angle. Then, holding the glass by its stem, tilt it over a white background to check the actual hue of the wine at the deepest point of the bowl and the gradation of colour towards the edge. Note the tell-tale intensity of colour at the rim. Finally hold the glass up to a light to judge its clarity and brightness.

Under the heading of 'Appearance' on p. 50, there is a detailed description of the various points to look for when examining a wine. The following examples of actual wines have been selected to illustrate a wide range of colour combinations rather than to represent every major wine district. They will help the reader to pinpoint the most significant areas of depth and hue. The seemingly endless number of variations that can occur are due to differences of district, grape, quality of vintage and age of wine and are part of the fascination that truly fine wines hold for the serious taster.

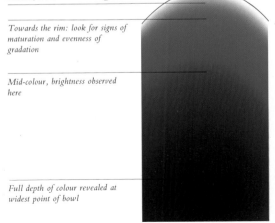

The intensity of colour at the rim or meniscus is indicative of richness, concentration and age

Towards the rim: look for signs of maturation and evenness of gradation

Mid-colour, brightness observed here

Full depth of colour revealed at widest point of bowl

COLOUR VARIATIONS

Immature Red Bordeaux

A classed-growth Médoc of
good vintage (sample drawn
after 1 year in cask)

*Fairly intense at rim – immature
purple or violet colour is clearly
visible*

*Good depth of colour maintained
from centre to edge*

*Deep mulberry colour, almost
opaque in centre*

Maturing Red Bordeaux

Top-class château of great
vintage, beginning to mature
after 9 years

*Outer rim red-brown indicating
some maturity*

*Fine claret red, the initial
youthful purple now lost*

*Still deep in colour but no longer
opaque*

Fine Mature Red Bordeaux

Perfectly mature 26-year-old
claret of excellent château and
outstandingly elegant vintage

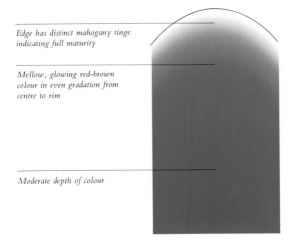

*Edge has distinct mahogany tinge
indicating full maturity*

*Mellow, glowing red-brown
colour in even gradation from
centre to rim*

Moderate depth of colour

Overmature Red Bordeaux

A good château and good
vintage but after 55 years
beginning to deteriorate

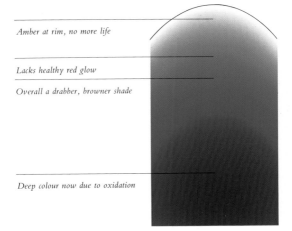

Amber at rim, no more life

Lacks healthy red glow

Overall a drabber, browner shade

Deep colour now due to oxidation

Five-year-old White Graves

Produced by a château known for both its white and red wines

Most dry white wines have a colourless rim

Gradual thinning of colour

Pale lemon colour will deepen slightly with age

Maturing 8-year-old Sauternes

From one of the top châteaux, a classic wine of a good, medium-weight vintage

Yellow tapers off to a virtually colourless rim

Appealing rich yellow colour

Initially deeper in colour than dry whites, sauternes becomes darker as it matures

Mature Great Sauternes

From the greatest of all the
Sauternes châteaux, a very
good vintage, 12 years old,
approaching its peak but
capable of further development
with a long life ahead

*Beautifully graduated to the palest
yellow at rim*

*Looks rich and sweet: the colour
of 21-carat gold leaf*

*The initial bright yellow-gold is
now a deeper burnished gold*

Very Old Classic Sauternes

Just over 50 years old, a first–
growth Barsac of great vintage

*The bright yellow-gold colour
presses up against the meniscus*

*The rich, warm, amber-gold is
enhanced by candlelight, giving
the wine taffeta-like highlights*

*Beautiful, translucent old-gold
colour of a perfect wine*

Young Beaujolais

A year-old village wine of
some quality and very good
vintage. For early drinking

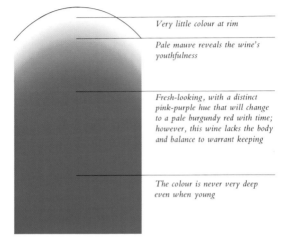

Very little colour at rim

*Pale mauve reveals the wine's
youthfulness*

*Fresh-looking, with a distinct
pink-purple hue that will change
to a pale burgundy red with time;
however, this wine lacks the body
and balance to warrant keeping*

*The colour is never very deep
even when young*

Maturing Burgundy

A 3-year-old Côte de Nuits, of
good vintage, starting to
mature

*The slightly purple rim indicates
immaturity; with age this will
become browner*

*Trace of red-brown near the edge
is a hint of development*

True burgundy red

*Reassuring depth of colour; other
burgundies of the same vintage
may be slightly deeper or paler*

Mature Burgundy

A 30-year-old Côte de Nuits,
of excellent vintage and from a
moderately good shipper

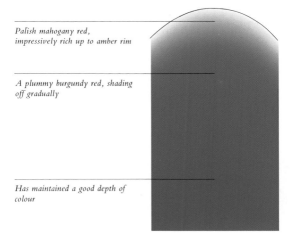

*Palish mahogany red,
impressively rich up to amber rim*

*A plummy burgundy red, shading
off gradually*

*Has maintained a good depth of
colour*

Very Old Burgundy

A 60-year-old, fully mature
grand cru burgundy of a classic
vintage

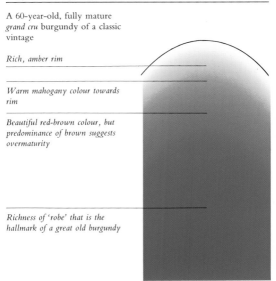

Rich, amber rim

*Warm mahogany colour towards
rim*

*Beautiful red-brown colour, but
predominance of brown suggests
overmaturity*

*Richness of 'robe' that is the
hallmark of a great old burgundy*

Manzanilla Sherry

Young, lightly fortified wine, best drunk freshly bottled. Dry and zestful

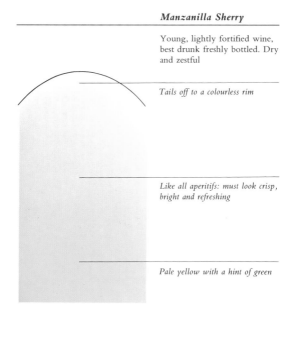

Tails off to a colourless rim

Like all aperitifs: must look crisp, bright and refreshing

Pale yellow with a hint of green

Amontillado

A good, commercial, medium-dry sherry

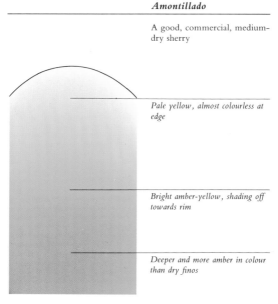

Pale yellow, almost colourless at edge

Bright amber-yellow, shading off towards rim

Deeper and more amber in colour than dry finos

Old-bottled Oloroso

A high-quality oloroso sherry,
cask-matured in Spain, bottled
in Bristol 25 years ago

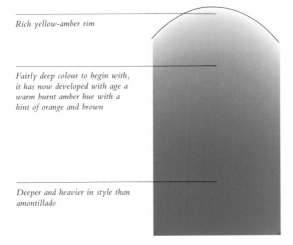

Rich yellow-amber rim

*Fairly deep colour to begin with,
it has now developed with age a
warm burnt amber hue with a
hint of orange and brown*

*Deeper and heavier in style than
amontillado*

Finest Old Brown Sherry

Old-fashioned style of sherry,
very sweet and concentrated in
flavour after considerable age
in cask

*Pronounced amber-brown rim
with faint green tinge*

*Suffused with orange towards the
edge*

*Rich, 'toasted', translucent brown,
indicative of age and quality*

*Deep brown, often opaque at
centre*

Immature Vintage Port

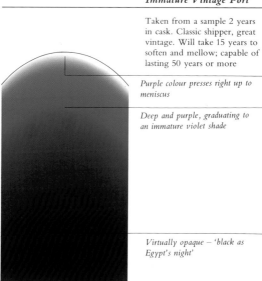

Taken from a sample 2 years in cask. Classic shipper, great vintage. Will take 15 years to soften and mellow; capable of lasting 50 years or more

Purple colour presses right up to meniscus

Deep and purple, graduating to an immature violet shade

Virtually opaque – 'black as Egypt's night'

Fine Ruby Port

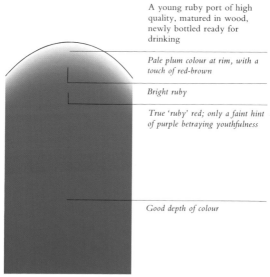

A young ruby port of high quality, matured in wood, newly bottled ready for drinking

Pale plum colour at rim, with a touch of red-brown

Bright ruby

True 'ruby' red; only a faint hint of purple betraying youthfulness

Good depth of colour

Mature Vintage Port

A great vintage from a top
shipper; shipped in cask and
bottled after 2 years; matured
in bottle for 30 years. Ready
now but will keep

Pale orange-brown rim

*No sign of purple anywhere;
instead it is a warm tawny red*

*Totally different from a young
vintage port: the initial opacity is
lost, together with a considerable
fading and softening of colour*

Finest Old Tawny Port

Matured in wood, then bottled
in Oporto at its peak of
maturity. Perfect now

Pale, amber-tawny rim

*Genuine old tawnies, aged in
wood, are usually fairly pale with
gentle gradation of colour*

*Warm, tawny-red with a ruddy
glow, sometimes with a slight
orange hue*

Young Rhine Wine

A 3-year-old Riesling Spätlese of very good vintage from a top vineyard in the Palatinate district

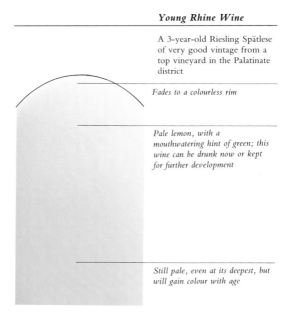

Fades to a colourless rim

Pale lemon, with a mouthwatering hint of green; this wine can be drunk now or kept for further development

Still pale, even at its deepest, but will gain colour with age

Mature Rhine Wine

A 26-year-old, great, fully ripe vintage, from a leading estate in Rheingau

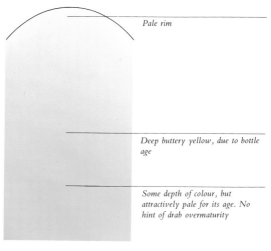

Pale rim

Deep buttery yellow, due to bottle age

Some depth of colour, but attractively pale for its age. No hint of drab overmaturity

Overmature White Burgundy

From a great and classic
vintage, but after 34 years it
has lost its initial zest,
becoming rather flabby

Insipid rim

*Colour of old straw, with a faint
orange tinge; dull, lacking sheen*

*Noticeable depth of colour; almost
drab, with a touch of brown*

Australian Muscat

An intensely sweet, fortified
dessert wine from northeast
Victoria, long aged in cask

*An intense, green-gold rim
indicates age and quality*

*Neither tawny nor ruby, it has a
warm russet colour, not found in
other wines*

Fairly deep and rich

Napa Valley Zinfandel

Almost a caricature of a great Californian red: a 3-year-old late-harvest Zinfandel, high in strength, slightly sweet and with a long life ahead

Colour rich to rim, with immature violet tinge

Deep blackberry hue: high alcoholic content and 'extract'

Virtually opaque, almost like young vintage port

Napa Cabernet-Sauvignon

A top vintage from a relatively new winery. At 5 years of age, it has a long future during which colour loss and changes will be very gradual

Intensely red at rim, indicative of 'extract' and quality

Initially opaque, it is now a translucent, finely graded shade of ruby red

Deep ruby at centre

Semi-mature
Châteauneuf-du-Pape

The big classic Rhône wines
are becoming increasingly rare;
this is a 10-year-old example
from one of the best vineyards

*The red-brown rim is the only
visual concession to maturity*

*Good, rich mid-red – still
youthful for its age*

*Depth of colour reflects high
alcoholic content, body and
'extract'*

Maturing Australian Red

A 4-year-old 'claret'-style wine
from one of the oldest-
established wineries in the
Barossa Valley

*Considerable purple intensity at
rim suggests richness, body and
immaturity*

*Still a distinct, somewhat youthful
plummy-purple colour*

*Noticeable 'hot-country' depth of
colour; probably has a high
alcoholic content*

Sercial Madeira

A standard commercial blend of *sercial* from an old-established madeira shipper. Has acquired some cask age, but does not improve in bottle. For immediate consumption

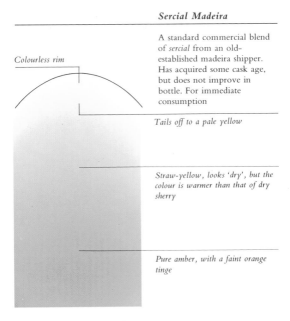

Colourless rim

Tails off to a pale yellow

Straw-yellow, looks 'dry', but the colour is warmer than that of dry sherry

Pure amber, with a faint orange tinge

Old Vintage Madeira

A 'straight' vintage from pure *bual* grapes, with at least 50 years in cask, 40 years in glass demijohns and about 15 years in bottle. Magnificent wine

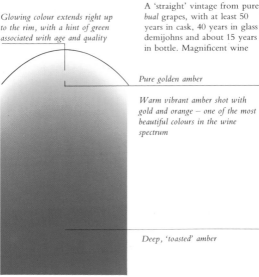

Glowing colour extends right up to the rim, with a hint of green associated with age and quality

Pure golden amber

Warm vibrant amber shot with gold and orange — one of the most beautiful colours in the wine spectrum

Deep, 'toasted' amber

VIII

THE USE OF WORDS

'When I use a word,' Humpty Dumpty said in a
rather scornful tone, 'it means just what I choose it to mean —
neither more nor less.'
Lewis Carroll
Alice's Adventures in Wonderland

Put quite bluntly, most people simply do not know how and where to start describing a wine, and many are reluctant even to express an opinion. Some, knowing more, are less shy; but do they really mean what they say, or is a familiar-sounding wine word being used just because it *is* familiar sounding, perhaps impressive? The odds are that it will not convey the speaker's intention.

Renewed thoughts on the use of words in relation to wine were stimulated by an interesting paper by Adrienne Lehrer.★ However, I was really shaken into action by contradictory statements about identical wines made by fellow Masters of Wine on a visit to the winelands of the Cape. It seemed to me that if experienced professionals, as well as untrained amateurs, could disagree on whether a wine was full, light or dry, or whatever, it was less likely to be a sensory problem than a semantic one: either carelessness in the use of words or alarming imprecision.

Clearly some guidance is needed.

Are words necessary?
It might justifiably be asked at this stage whether it is necessary to use words at all. Surely wine can be consumed, enjoyed and appreciated to the full without a word being said or written? There are several reasons for talking or writing about wine. Basically:
● to express a simple preference for one wine over another
● to communicate the style, quality, condition, etc. of a wine to someone else
● to increase the awareness of other tasters.

On what sort of occasion?
Tastings The context in which wine is tasted is all important. In the first chapter I mentioned different circumstances in which wine can be tasted, from the cask to the table. On each of these occasions a written or mental note would be made, possibly after discussion with the cellar-master or merchant (or whomsoever).

At the sort of tastings described in Chapter VI one would normally make notes, ranging from an abbreviated preferential tick or dismissive cross to more detailed descriptions.
Lectures A lecturer on wine has several responsibilities:
● to stimulate interest and enthusiasm
● to open the eyes of the audience by drawing attention to features they might not have noticed
● to select words which are evocative and meaningful
● to use words which can be clearly related to the wine being tasted by the audience

★'Talking about Wine' in the journal *Language*, Volume 51, Number 4 (1975), Committee of Linguistics, College of Liberal Arts, University of Arizona.

October 22 1981 David Peppercorn's 50th birthday dinner, London W.1

(Serena; David's parents; Deborah & Julian Jeffs; Liz & Peter Hasslacher; Daphne ~9)

**** '47	Veuve-Clicquot	(magnum)	Good colour for age. Rich gold. Lively	Lovely old straw bouquet	Medium dry leading to very dry, noticeably acid finish. Rich. Masterful
**** '59	Brauneberger Juffer Feine Spätlese	Licht. Prüm	medium yellow. Rich. Bright	Soft, mellow old Riesling. Rich vintage + bottle age	Medium - sweet, plump, even for a Mosel. Slight flash of acidity. Excellent with pêre
** '31	Château Latour	C.B. (re-corked at château)	Great classic German vintage. Very deep for '31 & poor vintage (Second bottle)	Old and dusty at first. Developed well in glass. Not as good. Looking unstable; acidity taking over	Dry, old and creaking. Flavoury but a little sour and unharmonious
**** '28	Ch. Léoville-Las-Cases	C.B	Fairly deep; fine mahogany tinge	Sweet, waxy, elegant St Julien bouquet	Dryish; medium body. Suave, lovely flavour. 129 refinement with 13 longevity. Exquisite aftertaste
**** '50	Ch. Coutet Barsac	Bottled in Margate, Osborne & Co	Deep-ish old gold. Slightly orange tinge. Demonstrates the quality of the '50 white Bordeaux and high standard of English bottling of Mosel	Sound, harmonious, crème brûlée bouquet	Medium-sweet (ie edging on a little Vanilla/crème. Crisp dry fruit. Lovely
***** '31	Quinta do Noval		Deep; virtually opaque	Sweet, full bodied. Complete, massive, concentrated fruit	Sweet, full bodied. Huge and still peppery. Liquorice. Length ---

The EVEREST of vintage port. Heavenly — 50 years of life ahead!

● when lecturing wine-trade students, to guide them in the use of words, particularly those long-tried and conventional terms which, when written, will be understood by an examiner or, equally, by a customer.

Selling wine It is fairly common practice for wine merchants to annotate their lists, describing the qualities of different types of wine, of vintages, even of individual wines. Similar eulogies will be conveyed by the salesman to the potential customer. It is much less difficult to use words in a selling context, possibly because the descriptions are qualitative and general, not analytical: pleasure-invoking adjectives, and opinions regarding readiness to drink, rather than specific descriptions. Perhaps, in the case of white wines, merely whether sweet or dry; reds, whether full-bodied or light.

At dinner parties There are many reasons for giving, or attending, a dinner party. If it is mainly a social event, grand or less formal, the purpose will be to impress or to entertain: the occasion and the people will take precedence over the fare. The food and the wine are likely to be relegated to a supporting role. The choice of wine will depend on appropriateness and price. It is not provided as a subject for discussion. Even so, if you are keen on wine there is no harm in making a discreet note.

However, if it is a food-and-wine occasion, the host will expect comments, even a discussion, though the level and intensity will depend as much on the knowledge and enthusiasm of the people present as the quality of fare. The point is: whether wines are discussed considerably or not at all will depend on the type of dinner, the guests and the intention. To pontificate on wine in a non-wine context is tactless; *not* to comment intelligently on wine in a wine-orientated context is a failure to rise to the occasion.

Great wine – for whom?

Arising out of my travels over the past few years it is abundantly clear that the vast majority of owners of fine and rare wines have a major concern; on what occasion, and for whom, shall their vinous treasures be opened? It is less a matter of expense than sheer waste, and the knowledge that once a cork is drawn, that's it. A fine picture can be looked at scores of times, and resold; a piece of silver can be admired for its beauty of craftsmanship, and still retain its intrinsic value. Apart from *haute cuisine*, great wine is the only work of art which has to be consumed in order to be appreciated. Thereafter its only value is a treasured memory.

It seems sensible, therefore, to keep the finest wines for dinner parties or tastings which will be attended by people who really appreciate them, or at the very least by like-minded convivial souls. Having gathered together fine wine and appreciative palates, host and guests alike are unlikely to be satisfied with grunts, nods and mere smacking of lips.

Choice of words

Fine wine demands to be talked about. Words are needed. There is a wide spectrum of words, but they more or less boil down to two categories: factual and fanciful. There is, I believe, a place for both.

When it comes to wine, facts very often turn out to be opinions. But let us not be put off by academic pedants. Better to fumble and stumble than not to try to express ourselves at all.

Terminology The arts and sciences, gardening and snooker, all have their own specialized words, often far more obscure than those used by wine-tasters, so why all the fuss, why the occasional snigger? It is extremely difficult to find words to describe taste, even more so bouquet, but one must try. One uses analogies and approximations. The most brilliant taster will be able to conjure up words which happen, at that moment, to fit, to illuminate, the wine under scrutiny. The experienced taster harnesses his imagination to vinous terminology.

Basic words At the end of this chapter I have extracted a short list of words which, if carefully (I avoid the word 'correctly') used, are meaningful to English tasters who have had a modicum of training and experience.

Fanciful words By all means let us indulge in flights of poetic expression, similes, flower analogies and so forth, but be careful about the context.

Unqualified and ambiguous words One taster will loosely describe a wine as 'full', another taster might disagree totally. The point here is that 'full', unqualified, can conjure up several meanings in other tasters' minds: full-coloured (deep), full-bodied (high alcohol and extract), full bouquet (well developed, very forthcoming), full-flavoured (positive, mouth-filling).

So adjectives like 'full' or 'light' should either be qualified or used in a distinctly recognizable context: colour, bouquet, weight in the mouth, style, flavour, etc. Words such as 'hot' and 'round' can have several meanings. A list of ambiguous words appear on p. 104.

Use of similes and analogies The French themselves, in writing and in speech, tend to be far more poetic than the English, their descriptions often roaming up a romantic path, associating wine with flowers, scents, exotic foods and the more delicate aspects of love-making. The English are generally more reticent, more terse and, let us be honest, often less imaginative. I find I cannot generalize about Americans. Their writing and talking depend on so many factors, from ethnic background to type of reader and audience. There *is* a tendency, in some quarters, to verbosity and polysyllables, many Americans preferring to use long words rather than clear simple expressions, but this is not confined to those who write, or speak, about wine. One could argue that likening a bouquet to violets or saying a taste is reminiscent of truffles is not very meaningful if the listener or reader is unfamiliar with the smell of one and the flavour of the other. Yet I believe it is quite defensible to do so; analogies add extra dimensions and help other tasters to identify and memorize facets.

There are instances where, at a dinner party of like-minded individuals, the sheer compatibility of guests, food and wines will spark off conversation of a high order. The possibility that a profusion of abstract similes, analogies, evocations, richly enlightening at the time, would, if recorded, sound pretty flat the next morning is immaterial.

A fine example of evocative writing, neatly bridging the gap between the French and English approach to wine, is demonstrated by the late André Simon. In the first issue of the *Quarterly Journal of the Wine and Food Society* he recorded what was to be the first of a series of memorable meals. It took place at the Hind's Head at Bray. At the end of the dinner the host, Barry Neame, asked André for his initial reaction to the wines. He answered that his 'first thoughts evoked memories of

Berkshire'. A 1926 Chablis – this was in 1934 – reminded him of 'the grace of the silver willow', the 1919 Montrachet 'of the stateliness of the Italian poplar', the 1920 Cheval-blanc 'of the magnificence of the purple beech' and the 1870 Lafite 'of the majesty of the Royal Oak'. But as to the brandy (an 1842 Roullet et Delamain) 'there was no tree with its roots in common clay to be mentioned in the same breath . . .'!

The wine snob

Out of a lesser man's mouth, with inappropriate wines, without the touch of real poetry and, above all, without imagination and understanding, André Simon's words would represent the quintessence of wine snobbery. Frankly, 'snob' is a term I try to avoid. But, alas, it is only too frequently used, equally by the ignorant and by the academic. As I believe the snob's main armoury is language, it is appropriate to raise the subject at this point.

If there is such a thing as a wine snob, he or she will have all the attributes of any other sort of snob: affectation and pretentiousness covering up the lack of everything that makes a person worthy of serious attention. The aristocrat of the table, the nature's gentleman of the cellar, the true *amateur*, the deeply knowledgeable, is rarely, if ever, a snob.

Those who are modest, undogmatic, who listen to others' views and are honest in their own opinions, should be safe from the brickbats of the envious and ignorant. Those who are knowledgeable about wine should merely be careful on what occasion and in whose company they air their opinions and display their scholarship.

The wine bore

People who say little or nothing are not bores, just boring. It is the man of words (woman equally) who is at risk. A great expert can be a bore, particularly if speaking out of context, being repetitive, pedantic, opinionated, never listening to others or merely intoning in a tedious, grinding, long-winded way.

The wine bore is the person who speaks about wine when no one is inclined to listen, or to the exclusion of all else. The answer is to try, which is not always easy, to talk about one's enthusiasm or business only in the presence of those who are interested, and, if possible, to anticipate the level of that interest.

Context of tasting

The trouble is, all those who talk about wine lay themselves wide open. If we talk of what we know not, to impress, we are wine snobs; if we talk of what we know, we are wine bores. Let us therefore forget these pejorative terms and concentrate on building up our knowledge, and on the correct use of words. 'Context' has cropped up several times in this book. It happens to be the crux of the problem. The *context* in which wine is tasted, and talked about, is of the greatest importance.

The occasion As stated earlier, tasting occasions, opportunities and settings vary. The same wine may be viewed in a different light, and one's impressions and notes can differ.

Time and timing Tiredness, a rushed tasting, will affect one's judgment and reduce the value of the tasting notes.

Lighting and colour The effects of natural and artificial lighting were discussed in Chapter V.★

Service of wine Wine served too warm or too cold, or tasted in too warm or too cold a room, will not taste the same. Wines served in one order might taste slightly different from the same wines served in another order.

Personal influences A dominant personality, or a dogmatic one, can make one's judgment waver. Try not to be diverted: rely on your own opinion.

I could go on. The point is that the senses, being delicate, are swayed by a multiplicity of outside factors. The impressions and the notes will reflect these; we must be conscious of influences, and if necessary, counter or allow for them. After all, we are only human!

Subjective or objective tasting

This brings me to a point which, I am sure, will be contentious. After more than 30 years of tasting and teaching I am convinced that to talk about, let alone claim, total objectivity – 'relating entirely to the external object' – in tasting is nonsense. Moreover, to be a subjective taster is nothing to be ashamed of. One can even argue that a subjective approach – 'arising out of the senses' – is the most enriching approach to *fine* wine. The problem is, as usual, to note or convey both subjective and objective impressions, using words which can be understood. The sole *object* of one's concentration should be the wine, but in the ultimate analysis 'I, the taster', am the final arbiter.

Judgment and taste thresholds

There are two areas in which judgment is required: at the commercial level and at the *amateur* (in the French sense). At the commercial level, a merchant, with or without formal training, will taste and use his judgment; will note and convey information about the wine to his customers. At wine festivals and shows, where wine is tasted competitively, the judges must work to a common approach and system of assessing wines. The more similar in quality and style the wines are, the more precisely the basis of judgment must be defined. When it comes to detecting small differences, particularly in wines of neutral character, the sensory thresholds (the level at which elements of smell and taste can be detected) of the judges are important. It would be sensible to test these; and it is possible to do so.†

Quantifying taste

I cannot subscribe to the dictum that, in effect, nothing is worth knowing unless it can be expressed numerically; indeed, in respect of fine wine I cannot help feeling that a preoccupation with numbers merely serves to divert the taster from the true appreciation of the manifold facets of quality and style.‡

Having said this I can see little harm in allocating marks to wines, so long as it is realized that a simple 'out-of-ten' (20 or a 100) score is only one taster's judgment of a given wine, in the

★Professor Puisais (Directeur du Laboratoire Départemental et Régional d'Analyses et des Recherches, Tours) has conducted experiments leading him to conclude that certain wall colours will make a wine taste sweeter or more acid.
†Refer to the several Amerine and Roessler works in the Appendix.
‡Emile Peynaud has more recently stated, I note with satisfaction, 'that which cannot be measured is often of greater significance than that which can'.

context of a range of wines, in given company, on a particular day. It will merely serve to underline and summarize impressions and notes. Allocating a simple numerical rating also obliges one to reach a conclusion.

Averaging scores

Beware: to take the average of the scores or marks of a number of tasters, particularly if they are many and varied in experience and ability, can be highly misleading. It can reduce to a blurred middle-of-the-road sector both outstandingly good and below-average, even faulty, wines. An overgenerous scorer will neutralize a highly critical one.

Statistical procedures

The French and American academics' partiality to algebra is altogether another thing. The object of the statistician is to reduce the chance element in tasting. In effect, one eliminates as far as possible all the conditions which induce the varying subjective impressions I have already referred to, and, after testing the tasters, analyses the results mathematically. I concede that with certain types of wine and in certain circumstances there is a case to be made, but it is generally beyond the level of knowledge and out of the area of interest of most wine lovers, in or out of the trade.

Summing up

Be honest with yourself. Try and express your own impressions and opinions but be particularly careful in your use of words if you need to note specific factors, convey them to a third person or recognize them again.

Frankly the subdivisions are infinite. One can argue endlessly about what words should be used. What might be acceptable to, and perfectly understood by, one person, may sound fatuous to another. There are no hard-and-fast rules. Words will vary from person to person, group to group; they will depend on usage, on teaching. Some will come into favour, some will fall out of favour.

In a social context, with good wines and like-minded people, loosen up: don't be afraid to express an opinion or a preference; let your imagination roam. Evocative comments help open up new vistas for others, and aid the overall appreciation and mental digestion of the wine. It is not so much precision that is required but a vital exchange of reactions and ideas, enabling so much more to be revealed, so much more to be gained.

In the final analysis, words should be used to illuminate and to enlighten; and they *must* be used as meaningfully as possible. If in doubt, refer to the following glossary. Check what *you* think you mean by what – let me be honest – *I* think I mean. You might not agree with all the definitions. At least they will provide food for thought. Lastly, try to use words in the correct context, and qualify them when necessary.

BASIC DESCRIPTIVE & DANGER WORDS

Below are listed basic descriptive words and expressions in the order of tasting of any red or white wine. Refer to the Full Glossary in Chapter XII for definitions.

———————————— Red Wines ————————————

Appearance

depth	very pale, pale, medium-pale, medium-deep, deep, very deep, opaque
colour/hue	purple, purple-rimmed, ruby, red, tile-red, brown-tinged, red-brown, mahogany
clarity	bright, dull, bitty, hazy, cloudy; light or heavy sediment

Nose or bouquet

condition	clean, unclean (sulphury, oxidized, etc.)
fruit	fruity, lacking fruit, vinous, varietal, named variety
development	dumb, immature, undeveloped, well developed, forthcoming, very mature, overmature
quality	poor, ordinary, good, fine, great, magnificent

Palate

apparent dryness	(noticeably) dry; slightly or unusually sweet (for a red wine); tannic
body	very light (VL)★, light (L), medium-light (ML), medium (M), full-bodied (F), heavy
tannin	marked, noticeably drying, mellow
acid	soft, lacking acidity, refreshing, marked acidity, overacid, tart, acetic
fruit, flavour	fruity, lacking fruit; vinous; very flavoury, lacking flavour (describe flavour – use analogies when appropriate)
development	well developed, very mature, mature, beginning to mature, undeveloped, 'green'
overall balance	well balanced, unbalanced
length and finish	long flavour, short; lingering, fine aftertaste

———————————— White Wines ————————————

Slight difference of emphasis, particularly regarding colour and sweetness:

Appearance

depth	colourless, very pale, medium, deep
colour/hue	green-tinged, yellow-green, yellow, straw, yellow-gold, gold, amber, deep gold, brown
clarity	star-bright, bright, dull, cloudy, bitty

Nose or bouquet

	more or less as for red wines

Palate

dry/sweet	bone-dry, dry, medium-dry, medium-sweet, sweet, very sweet
body, acidity, fruit, development, balance, finish	more or less as for red wines. Tannin is not normally a factor in white wines; acidity is more important, balancing sugar content

★I use abbreviations in my own notes. The possible confusion between initials is avoided by tasting, and using words, in a regular order and under appropriate headings. For example, under 'Palate', 'D, MF' indicates 'dry, medium-full bodied'. Other abbreviations I use: fl. (flavour), bal. (balance), Y (youthful/immature), V/A (volatile acidity), B/A (bottle-age), mat. (mature), ex. (excellent), t & a (tannin and acidity), etc.

WORDS USED IN THE DESCRIPTION OF WINE, BY CATEGORY

For ease of reference, I have listed here those words in common use, those which need qualifying, those to use with care and additional qualitative adjectives. For a full list of tasting terms and their definitions, refer to the glossary in Chapter XII.

─────────── **Words in common use** ───────────

acid/acidity	dry/medium-	refreshing
aroma	dry etc.	soft
balance/well-	fruity	sweet
balanced	grapey	tannin, tannic
bouquet	hard	tough
clean	harsh	vinegary
	poor	watery

Words in common use which
─────────── **should be used in a qualified context** ───────────

aftertaste	flat	ordinary
big	full	peppery
bland	heavy	positive
body	light	rich
bright	little	round
character	long	sour
coarse	mature/maturity	strong
dull	meaty	varietal
fat	medium	weak
fine	neutral	youthful
finish		

─────────── **Words to use precisely or with care** ───────────

astringent	forthcoming	robust
baked	green	rough
bite	hot	sharp
bitter	iron	smoky
corked	maderized	stalky
dumb	mouldy	tang/tangy
earthy	nutty	tart
extract	oxidized	vinous
feminine	penetrating	woody
flabby	piquant	zesty/zestful
flinty	pungent	

─────────── **Additional qualitative descriptions** ───────────

aromatic	mellow	silky
breed, well bred	metallic	smooth
complex	musty	spicy
distinguished	noble	subtle
elegant	perfumed	supple
finesse	powerful	unripe
flowery	raw	velvety
fragrant	ripe	vinosity
insipid	scented	well developed
luscious	sensuous	yeasty

IX

HOW TO TASTE –
A PRACTICAL RECAPITULATION

*I am tempted to believe that smell and taste are
in fact but a single composite sense, whose laboratory is the mouth
and its chimney the nose.*
Brillat-Savarin
The Physiology of Taste, 1825

So far I have given the reader a good deal of background detail;
how the senses work, the elements which make up the tasting
process, and characteristics of regions, grapes, etc. The organization of tastings and the use of words have also been dealt with.
What I propose to do now is to summarize the act of tasting:
what precisely to look for, how to sniff and taste effectively and
what factors to bear in mind.

To start with, white wines tend to be less complex than reds:
the colour variations are narrower and less significant, the
aroma of a young white wine has an immediacy, is more readily
detectable, whereas the bouquet of a red evolves more slowly
and subtly. On the palate whites tend to have a simpler
counterpoint of sweetness and acidity, fruit and measurable
length, whilst reds are less of an open book, with alcohol and
tannins adding to their complexity.

UNDER THE HEADING APPEARANCE

The two main elements are depth and the actual hue or colour.
Secondary factors are clarity and viscosity. Here is how to set
about spotting them.

Depth

Assuming we have the correct sort of tasting glass, a white-
topped table and suitable lighting, previously described, the
depth of colour is observed by leaving the glass on the table and
looking down at an angle of 45° or from immediately above.
The variations in the depth of white wine is slight and relatively
unimportant. The depth of red wine *is* important and significant, a pale colour usually indicates lightness of body and
extract (though some fine burgundies with fairly high alcohol
content can be misleadingly pale), a deep colour foreshadows a
fuller-bodied wine, and a very deep, virtually opaque quality
will be indicative of high alcohol content and extract and
probably much tannin and fruit. The depth of colour can be
controlled by vinification, but in classic districts like Bordeaux a
deep colour generally indicates a good vintage, and conversely,
a week feeble colour a poor vintage. (Hot sun thickens the skins
which provide this red pigment; warmth creates, through the
leaves, the sugar content which converts into alcohol. So, in a
good year, after a hot sunny summer and early autumn, the
wine produced will have a deep, intense colour and high
alcohol content: the hotter the sun the darker and more
alcoholic the wine. Lack of both sun and warmth, usually
associated with cloudy, cold and wet weather results in thin
skins, low sugar converting to low alcohol, and pale colour.)

Colour or hue

Pick up the glass by the stem, tilt it over the white table top and, from above, observe the colour at the deepest part of the bowl and its gradation to the rim.

White wine Notice the hint of green in young dry whites, particularly from northerly wine districts like the Moselle and Sancerre; the more positive yellow pigment of a ripe *chardonnay* from Meursault or the Hunter Valley; the already yellow-gold shades of young dessert wines and the deeper yellows, golds and ambers resulting from mature bottle-age.

Red wine A bright purple rim indicates immaturity, a plummy red the transition stage and, before the red-brown of maturity sets in, a no man's land which I describe as 'on the turn'. Note the rich mahogany rim of an old claret and watch out for the telltale drab brown of one which is too old and oxidized.

Colour, incidentally, is the most accurate measure of the maturity of red wine.

Clarity, brightness, limpidity

Pick up the glass by the stem and hold it up to a light.

A fine wine in a healthy condition seems to have that extra sheen, rather like the bloom on a perfect peach. A lacklustre appearance will usually indicate a lacklustre wine. Slight bittiness may be due to careless bottling and is usually of little importance, as are pieces of cork, the result of the corking machine or one's own careless cork pulling. Cloudiness, a slightly milky, blue or orange hue indicates a fault.

Viscosity, legs and beads

Keep the base of the glass on the table and rotate it, swirling the wine up the sides of the glass. Observe the way the ring of liquid slips down and forms legs or tears. For their significance *see* p. 54.

At the same time see if there are any telltale beads round the rim of the wine, tiny bubbles which, in a young white wine and some young reds, indicate the presence of carbon dioxide which will give a *spritzig* prickle or *pétillance* in the mouth; in an old red wine it is more likely a sign of cracking up.

UNDER THE HEADING NOSE OR BOUQUET

Again, rotate the base of the glass to rinse with wine the maximum inner surface area of the glass, arousing the wine and helping it to release its volatile ethers.

The next movement is to pick up the glass by the stem and just waft it under the nose. It is essential to give one's fullest concentration to this in order not to miss the vital first impression. Just lightly inhale and note whether the wine is clean and fresh, has a distinctive varietal (grape) aroma, shows youthful acidity, or mellow age.

By no means all that a wine has to reveal is yielded or conveyed by that first impression but it sometimes triggers off an immediate recognition. It is certainly the most evocative stage. And it is the first impression which, hopefully, will capture and encapsulate the fleeting volatile elements of the wine's make-up. Emile Peynaud with refreshing simplicity describes volatile substances as 'those capable of escaping from the glass or disappearing in the mouth'. They are easy, superficially, to spot but very difficult to analyse, extremely important in relation to quality and, to quote Peynaud again, 'give the wine its personality'.

Next, give another gentle swirl, hold the wine to the nose and this time give it quite a few short, sharp sniffs. Whilst doing this try to sort out each element: the fruit, perhaps a noticeable grape variety, the acidity – mouth-puckering malic, the cooking apple smell of unripe green grapes; the pleasant mouthwatering tartaric acid; the high-toned faintly vinegary whiff of too high volatile acidity.

Beware: if you sniff too protractedly over a short period of time the nose will become anaesthetized. The same applies to really deep long sniffs. The net result in each case will be a diminution of smell.

Sometimes a very young red wine yields little on the nose. A leathery smell indicates the presence of considerable tannin, a pepperiness high alcohol content. Deeper sniffs will detect and draw out underlying latent richness and fruit.

A mature white wine of a good vintage will have a soft, fragrant, honey-like bouquet. A fine mature claret a well-knit mellow, warm brick smell which will develop in the glass to a rich, wholemeal-biscuity fragrance. But a magnificently opulent bouquet sometimes serves to disguise the structure of an old wine which may be falling apart.

Young wines have raw component parts which can, in effect, be separated, i.e. individually detected. As wines mature, those component parts blend together, losing their individual identities, becoming a complete, homogeneous fragrance – but not by any means the same: burgundy and claret, Rheingau and Anjou, each will have its own character, weight, style.

UNDER THE HEADING PALATE OR TASTE

For the experienced taster, the wine in the mouth will largely confirm what the eye has seen and judged and the nose smelled and assessed.

Take a sip, a reasonable mouthful. Notice the entry: here any sweetness will be detected. Draw in air as the wine crosses the tongue. This will help the aromatic elements of taste fill the mouth. If at a tasting, spit out, otherwise swallow, noting various facets as it crosses the palate, its length and finish.

Note the taste elements in a logical order:

Sweetness

Perhaps the most important feature of a white wine, and certainly the first to be noticed. Is it dry, i.e. totally lacking sweetness, slightly sweet or very sweet?

Virtually all red wines are fully fermented out, leaving little or no residual sugar. So the dryness/sweetness factor is not important: red wines are basically dry. Having said this, a certain softness and slight sweetness is noted when a red wine has been made from fully ripe grapes, of a particularly good vintage in Bordeaux or Burgundy, or from a hot sunny wine area. This is partly due to a minute amount of residual sugar but mainly, I believe, from the unusually high level of ethyl alcohol, which gives an impression of sweetness.

Sweetness should be judged on entry not at the back of the mouth as the acid content of the wine can have a masking effect or, conversely, may exaggerate the dryness. Wines with naturally high acidity, like madeira and some German dessert wines, need sweetness to be palatable, as strawberries need sugar.

Acidity

Acidity makes one cluck one's tongue. An agreeable degree of tartaric acid will give the wine a pleasant, refreshing quality. To me, acidity is the nervous system of a wine, for apart from its effect in the mouth it is one of the essential elements, a cornerstone, without which the wine will not keep, and without which it will be flat and dull. Acidity gives the wine finish. It also counterbalances the natural sugar content of sweet wines.

Too much acidity, raw unripe acidity, upsets the balance, tastes tart, draws in the cheeks. There are various sorts of acidity and many words used to describe degrees and effects of acidity – such as acetic, sharp, tart, green, sour – listed in the Full Glossary of Tasting Terms.

Body, weight, alcohol

Is the wine light and insubstantial in the mouth or is it heavy, massive, mouth filling? The dominating factor is alcohol. 11° G.L. or 11% by weight or volume, more or less the same, feels light, is light: for example mosels. Medium weight will probably be in the 12% area, say a moderately good claret of a moderately good vintage. Full-bodied is 13% or more: a red Corton or classic Châteauneuf-du-Pape. But alcohol does not travel alone. A full-bodied young red wine will also be loaded with tannin; it will have extract, in short, substance. But alcohol is the wine's backbone.

Tannin

As this is derived from skins and pips during fermentation, also from long storage in small oak casks, tannin is a major element in the structure of red wines (white wines are fermented without skins and pips and sometimes spend little or no time in wooden casks).

Tannin dries the mouth. In young wines it is also bitter, but this ameliorates with age. It is essential to have high alcoholic content to balance, with its sweetness and warmth, the astringency of a substantial tannic content. Where the alcoholic content and extract is comparatively low, as with young beaujolais, the tannin is exposed and often leaves a bitter, tinny taste in the mouth.

Fruit, wood and other flavours

Sugars, acids, alcohols and tannins are, perhaps, the basic structural elements. Happily the flavour of wine is supplemented by a myriad of other trace elements, volatile, fixed, derived from the fruit itself, from the minerals taken from the soil, from the process of fermentation, the yeasts, from the wood, even from the air.

A lot of spicy and aromatic flavours (and smells, for they are linked) are directly attributable to a particular cause. For example, vanilla is from ethyl vanilline, the principal odour of oak wood; leather from tannin. But by far the most smells and tastes are described by analogy, the closest resemblance to the wine in the mouth. Yet all are there for a particular physical or chemical reason.

That is why the taster should first of all try hard to recognize smells and tastes such as tobacco, pine or petroleum, caramel, crusty bread, liquorice, pepper, cinnamon, and note the wine, its origin, age, grape variety, so that one can link a smell and a place, a soil, a method of wine-making, a hot year. The combination of these smells and tastes often results in something indefinable. Add an element, try to take it away, and the whole ensemble crumbles. This is the mystery, and the challenge of wine.

The taster should not be afraid to try and put into words the immediate impact of the smell and taste of a wine no matter how fanciful these may sound. Let the wine do the speaking, you do the translating.

──────── **Balance, finesse – the facets of quality** ────────

By balance we mean that the interwoven component parts are in equilibrium: not just that the acidity balances the tannin, that the alcohol is sufficient to support both, but that the subtler, volatile and often evasive elements add to the sum total, not detract, add character without being intrusive.

A young wine can be balanced despite its lack of development, but only a fully mature wine will have the softness, yet firmness, delicacy with strength, length without attenuation, unfolding and revealing the more one noses and tastes.

Length is a measure of quality; the time the flavour takes to cross the mouth; fragrant intensity, filling the mouth with flavour; the aftertaste, the persistence of flavour and fragrance after the wine has been swallowed.

A poor wine might well have a raw, coarse texture, lack of positive flavour and a grubby, unclean end-taste. An ordinary wine comes into the mouth with no particular impact, has a neutral, faintly winey flavour which disappears via a short insipid end. A good wine will have a positive entry, positive flavour – a beginning, middle and end. A fine wine has length, possibly a silky texture, mouth filling yet delicate flavour, good length, crisp finish and a lingering after taste. A great wine is a fine wine with extra dimensions and, like a kaleidoscope, presents the taster's nose and palate with extraordinary changing patterns.

──────── **Making your own tasting notes** ────────

Try different ways of expressing in words the qualities of the same wine, first noting the basic elements: *deep purple/low-keyed nose/dry, full, tannic, unready*. Then expand, for example: *deep, opaque at the centre, immature purple rim*. Nose: *bouquet undeveloped but underlying aroma, merlot dominating. Will develop.* Palate: *hint of ripeness on entry but overall dry with substantial tannin and acidity. Full-bodied, high alcoholic content, rich extract, good length.* Conclude: *drinkable in five years, possibly fully developed in 10, sound mature lifespan up to 20 years from the date of tasting.* And what about a numerical rating, say 17/20 for intrinsic quality and future promise. If all this is too much, then at the very least: '*deep, young, will be good.*'

A last word of advice: try and gear your notes to match the type and quality of wine. It is fatuous to dream up an elaborate description of a wine whose sole virtue is a bargain price allied to modest drinkability. Conversely it is a tragic waste not to notice, and note, the beautiful appearance, fragrant nose and lovely taste of something really special.

The palate, like the eye, the ear, or touch, acquires with practice various degrees of sensitiveness that would be incredible were it not a well ascertained fact.

T. G. Shaw
Wine, the Vine and the Cellar, 1863

There are, I believe, two general but little-understood points concerning tasting ability, and they are related. First, the more one has tasted, the less clear-cut may be one's reactions and the less dogmatic one's pronouncements. This is because the experienced taster (almost always a professional) has been exposed to such a wide range of closely related smells and tastes, and has met with so many exceptions to the rules. The corollary is an easily noted one: that the beginner and amateur, having fresh perception and an uncluttered vinous memory, is frequently more certain of him or herself and sometimes more accurate in identification.

Second, a point which may probably be widely accepted but that is rarely admitted: successful 'guessing-game' experts almost always perform in the comparatively limited field of very fine wines and great vintages, the characteristics of which stand out in sharp black and white, compared with the half-tones of middle-quality wines or the bleak wash of the *ordinaires*. It is not uncommon for the highest scorers to be amateurs, for their greatest performances are usually set in an even more limited (however excellent) context, that of their own and their friends' cellars.

I do not wish to belittle the seasoned and discerning amateur palates, or spoil their fun. On the contrary, without such enthusiastic and enquiring attitudes, without lay scholarship, the precarious incentive to produce such wines would waver, to everyone's loss. I merely make these points to keep things in perspective.

Having cleared the ground, I would like to pursue the subject of tasting 'blind'.

Tasting blind

It is my firm opinion (one of the few these days unwhittled by doubts!) that to assess the qualities of a wine by tasting it completely blind, without any hint of what it might be, is the most useful and salutary discipline that any self-respecting taster can be given. It is not infrequently the most humiliating. The first thing it does is to concentrate the thoughts, and expose fresh and unprejudiced senses to the problem of analysing the colour, bouquet and flavour. To know what the wine is before one starts to taste is like reading the end of a detective novel first; it satisfies the curiosity but dampens the interest.

The occasion . . . Should blind tastings and guessing games be conducted at the dinner table? This is perhaps the most vexed question of all. I am sure that my colleagues in the British wine trade, particularly fellow Masters of Wine, will be the first to agree that it is one of the hazards of their occupation to be expected to perform before an anonymous-looking glass of wine and before only too un-anonymous and hideously expectant hosts and fellow guests: to pronounce vineyard, vintage and the name of the cellar-master in 10 seconds flat. It is not that it *cannot* be done, even in this time. It can, but only in rare and exceptional circumstances, and I exclude all known methods of cheating, like bribing the butler. The point is that unless there is an immediate and quite positive click of recognition, the only alternative is an extremely elaborate round-the-houses process of elimination, an intellectual exercise that takes time and may well be acutely boring for those waiting and watching. At a dinner party, particularly, the surest way of offending one's hostess is to undergo these mental contortions, letting one's meal go cold, and possibly even delaying subsequent courses.

. . . and the company Broad-minded professionals do not mind making fools of themselves in the company of others in the business. At least, they reassure themselves, their friends in the trade *know* how really difficult it is to identify wines, and they all have the comforting knowledge of their common manifold blunders. It is another thing to be exposed before, and caught out by, amateurs – perhaps their own customers – who simply do not understand the complexity and problems involved.

Dinner party tastings

I personally subscribe to blind tasting, at least of the principal wines, at a dinner party, but only on the following conditions:
● that the occasion is an appropriate one – good and carefully planned wines with appropriate food
● that the company is like-minded, otherwise the whole thing becomes a bit tedious and unbalanced; off-putting for expert and nonexpert alike
● that reasonable time is allowed for thinking about the wine; the service of wine and food must be timed to accommodate this. Nothing is more irritating and fatuous, in my opinion, than for a host to say 'What is it?' and then blurt out the answer before anyone has had a chance properly to examine the wine
● that the length of time is not dragged out and that no one is forced to a complete and final answer if it is not naturally forthcoming. Indeed, in mixed (not just 'genders', but professional and lay) company I think it probably tactless of the host to try to extract nearest answers in a competitive manner. If people want to be sporting, let them have a go. (This can be a good thing, for one is stimulated into thinking along fresh lines by hearing other people's reactions, and one finds perhaps a new point of view engendered.) It should be remembered, on the other hand, that some people can no more guess wines in public than they can stand on a table and sing.

The dinner-party host has peculiarly difficult responsibilities. There is a danger of two extremes that can be disheartening and deadly, respectively. Disheartening if beautiful wines are produced and not noticed or commented on at all; deadly if too much of a rigmarole is made of the occasion. Even variations in the middle range can be unsatisfactory. It is little satisfaction for a wine-loving guest to enjoy the wine but not to know what it is. The very least that should be provided is a small menu card with the wines listed, to be taken away by the interested guest. Quite frankly, I carry a little note card and make notes furtively or blatantly depending on how well I know the host.

Menu and wine cards

How does one provide a menu card without revealing in advance the names of the wines? There are at least two ways.

One is to provide a small folded card with a seal. When the seal is broken, the list of wines is revealed inside. (I first came across this, charmingly done, by that most articulate of wine lovers, Tony Alment, one of that excellent breed of civilized medical men who seem to be the universal backbone of wine-loving fraternities.) The other is a variation I occasionally use, slightly more elaborate in that it reveals the identity of each wine in turn. I write the menu on the left-hand side of a stiff card, and the matching list of wines, well spaced, on the right. Each wine name is covered with a finger of paper held in place by a paper clip. Those who cannot wait can quietly remove the covers. Those who want to rise to the challenge and persist until they have exhausted their memory banks can do so without keeping everyone in suspense.

It is nice to be able to arrive, by deduction, at a district or vintage. But I believe the main benefit of not knowing the wine in advance, even at a dinner party, to be this powerful concentration of thought and appreciative judgment which is, for the professional, a good discipline and, for the amateur, a continual test of discernment.

Before leaving tasting mystique and expertise, I would like to comment on two interesting facets of blind tasting.

First impressions

One is the subconscious, evocative memory that enables a taster, presumably highly sensitive to smells and tastes, to reach a perfect, or at least remarkably accurate, answer to a wine tasted blind. The value of first impressions is well known to tasters but its true significance is less well understood. As we have seen from Chapter IV on the physical aspects of tasting, the sense of smell, though often a Cinderella in development, is primitive and primal, and has the power of recalling a total experience from the memory, seemingly without the intervention of positive thought.

What is most frequently *not* comprehended is that if the memory-brain does not instinctively and immediately produce an intelligible reaction, the reliance on this for the wine in question must be abandoned, and conscious reasoning must begin.

Working it out

This second approach is totally opposite to the reflex action of the first impression; it requires the exercise of determined intellectual effort; the use of eyes, nose and palate to deduce the answer that the nerve cells and memory failed to conjure up at first go. I personally, at this stage, try to detect the grape used, the regional characteristics and work out a rough age-bracket; then, by the process of elimination, arrive backwards at the answer, or, at any rate, at an intelligent approximation of district and vintage, with a definite opinion of quality. All this takes time and patience. The results are rarely as spectacular as those produced by the evocative memory. Furthermore it may well bore the bystander, unless the reasoning is concise and thought out aloud to sustain interest. These important methods and techniques are dealt with below in greater detail.

No cheating!

The very last word on this subject is an appeal for honesty, tempered with consideration. Cheating and short cuts in the tasting game are self-defeating. The true taster puts his blinkers on, is honest with himself, and is not influenced and led astray by others. On the other hand, the pursuit of zealous tasting expertise should only be pursued in appropriate company, and then only with discretion; otherwise the whole thing becomes a bore.

APPRECIATION, RECOGNITION AND DEDUCTION

Having covered first principles, the senses, the approach to tasting and, broadly, those elements which give rise to taste, the time has come to dig a little deeper.

Tasting is not just an isolated theoretical exercise: it is usually an assessment of physical attributes in relation to a particular wine or wines, with a specific end in view (*see* p. 7). It may well have one of the following purposes:

● to assess the quality, state of development and possibly the value of a *known* wine

● to assess the relative quality and value of a known *type* of wine – possibly one of a range of similar or even identically named wines

● to identify, from its physical taste characteristics, the style, region, quality and maturity of an *unknown* wine.

We might even reduce the taster's problems to a basic two:

● knowing the name and full details of the wine, to judge its true qualities, etc. This boils down to *appreciation* and *assessment*

● knowing little or nothing about the wine, to find what it is, from an accurate assessment of its characteristics, by tasting alone. This is encompassed by two words: *recognition* and *deduction*.

Before embarking, however, I must stress that what follows must be seen in the context of a relaxed and informal group of like-minded *amateurs* (in the French sense) concentrating their attentions upon the merits of vintage wines. I am not writing about clinical laboratory tests to measure tasting thresholds, to isolate elements, to detect and quantify small differences in new wines made from experimental vines: these worthy endeavours we can leave to viticultural schools and oenological colleges.

Equally out of court are those formally – and often excellently – organized tasting competitions, interdistrict and international, where judges sit in splendid isolation to award medals to the best commercial entries. I am not trying to belittle either approach, though I confess I am confused and bored with some of the scientific approaches to sensory evaluation, with their emphasis on methodology, triangular tests, random numbers and abstruse mathematical formulae. Awarding gold medals can take on nationalistic or political overtones; some are like beauty contests, when it appears to the disinterested onlooker that the really lovely girls have stayed at home. The fact of the matter is that truly fine and great wines are not entered for such competitions, and if they were they would probably be wasted in such mediocre company. (These remarks do not apply to Australia where State wine competitions are immaculately organized and taken seriously by producer and public alike.)

——— **APPRECIATION AND ASSESSMENT** ———

At its most elementary level, appreciation manifests itself in a positive liking (or not liking) for a wine, whether at a tasting or at a dinner party. At the same level, discrimination is expressed by a preference for one wine amongst a group of wines. This is known as the hedonistic approach.

Wine merchants often find that even people fairly new to wine can be quite discriminating. Given two or three wines to taste, the customer will often express a marked preference for the best-quality wine of a group, price notwithstanding. However, the layman falters in trying to express the degree of quality, and in sifting and describing the individual characteristics which, in combination, have awakened his natural taste instincts.

Without wishing to be condescending, what I am trying to say is that appreciation and simple discrimination are relatively easy. The next stage, assessment, is more complex and requires some background knowledge and tasting experience. Take one very important element, quality, for example. Quality is always relative. Even the best Yugoslav Riesling will be on a lower quality plane than a good classic Rheingau such as a Rauenthaler Wieshell Riesling Spätlese; the best sparkling Loire wine rates lower than a good *grande marque* champagne; and the best unblended beaujolais is below the peak of a *grand cru* Côte de Nuits. One has to know the relative quality strata before one begins.

There is a whole kaleidoscope of tastes (and smells) that emanate from the physical characteristics of grape varieties, soil and climatic influences, wine-making techniques and effects of age (see Chapter II). They reveal style, areas and maturity as well as quality. The greater one's understanding of all these factors, the more accurate and rapid will be one's assessment and final pronouncement.

—— RECOGNITION AND DEDUCTION ——

Imagine that you are in the position where you are confronted with a glass containing an unknown wine. The steps which follow – the processes of recognition and deduction – are perhaps the most difficult a taster ever has to contend with. He will have to bring to bear *all* his critical tasting faculties and knowledge.

Guessing is not allowed. Or is it? Let's not be too dogmatic, for there is surely only a fine dividing line between the inspired guess and split-second recognition: both may stem from a subconscious signal from the evocative memory. However, what usually happens is that we are baffled and taunted by a half-familiar smell or taste that evades recognition. It remains on the tip of the tongue, literally in this case, and the harder we try, the less is revealed.

If there *is* failure of recognition at this stage, the only solution is to back out, start again and attempt deduction by a systematic examination of taste characteristics. This needs not just a good palate and a detailed knowledge of regions and vintages, but the ability to link the reactions of the former with the recollections of the latter. This is, unhappily, as difficult as it sounds. There are, however, two useful techniques to bring to bear: elimination and bracketing.

—— *Deduction by elimination* ——

The technique of elimination entails a mental exercise. Take the most positively identified characteristics of the wine, compare them with the known characteristics of other wines, and cross off those that do not remotely match up. In other words, first eliminate all the obvious wines it *cannot* be; then consider those it *could* be; finally, deduce what it *must* be. This simple and effective method can be used to arrive at the grape variety, style and geographical area; even the district and vineyard. It is also useful to confirm or strengthen opinions previously half-held.

Method What happens in practice is this: one picks up the glass of unknown wine and examines first its appearance, bouquet and flavour, sifting the normal, straightforward or classic from the unusual or 'foreign'.

Take its appearance first of all. Is it unusually deep (this applies to either red or white) or abnormally pale (red mainly)? Is it strikingly young and purple, or 'sear and yellow'? Is it star-bright or murky or slightly *pétillant*? The important thing is not just to notice these factors but to work out what might cause them. For example, unusual depth of colour in a red wine might be due to a fine hot vintage year in a temperate area like Bordeaux, or might indicate its origin in a sun-baked section of the Rhône valley, or from a particularly hot region like the irrigated areas of South Australia, California or the Cape. It could also arise from the vinification – a long fermentation which extracts a good deal of colour from the skins. With unusually pale-coloured wines the reverse might apply. All these will be clues, pointers. It is vital in the early stages *not* to jump to conclusions, but to leave the tracks open, passing on to the bouquet and then to the taste for a further crystallization of impressions, and then on to the final confirmation. So, I repeat, get as many clues and leads from the appearance as possible; leave doubts hanging in the air and then pass on to the bouquet.

With bouquet, once again one looks for any unusual or outstanding characteristics. First of all, whether there is a distinctive grape aroma and whether it is from a classic region or not. If it is pronounced, and you can recognize the grape, the areas where this grape is never grown can be eliminated. Incidentally, strength of bouquet, in the sense of fullness and forthcomingness is not the sole criterion, for a fine classic grape aroma can be subdued, even scarcely noticeable, particularly when the wine is young and undeveloped. What one is really looking for is clarity and purity of character. The more indeterminate, muddy and neutral the smell, the poorer the quality.

The most important thing of all is to realize that the combination of appearance and nose can provide many if not most of the clues to a wine's identity. By spotting the main characteristics of each and eliminating all that the wine *cannot* be, one's conclusions can then be confirmed on the palate; or one is left with likely alternatives that remain for the palate finally to sort out and decide.

Confirmation In what way can the palate aid and confirm? First of all, consider the major taste factors which are noted on the palate: sweetness (in white wine, mainly); the degree of tannin, acidity and alcohol; the extract; the continuity of varietal characteristics (i.e. flavour to match the grape aroma); finesse, breed and, above all, length and intensity of flavour and finish – in short, quality. It is the linking of these taste factors to the colour and smell which should firmly anchor the total impression and lead one straight, or more safely by elimination, to a logical conclusion.

It will be obvious now, if it wasn't before, that one can only eliminate on a broad 'taste front' by having a wide knowledge to match; on a narrow front by having a detailed knowledge. Take heart, for though considerable tasting experience is desirable, it is surprising how much can be achieved by limited experience aided by some theoretical knowledge of grape, district and age characteristics. By constantly reading wine books and articles one can, over a period, gain knowledge of what certain types of wine should taste like, and link the recollection of these characteristics to the actual taste of the wine in the glass. Indeed, I shall go one stage further and say that it is perfectly possible to deduce what a wine is even though one has never tasted it, or its type before, simply by recognizing taste characteristics one has read or heard about. It would be rash for the taster in such circumstances to say that the wine *is* from such and such a vineyard; better to conclude that it *might well be*. Indeed, to be dogmatic at all in the field of tasting is both risky and tiresome.

What to expect Now one of the difficulties facing the keen wine lover is finding out what a wine *should* taste like. Few of the many otherwise excellent books on wine actually help here. Nevertheless, if you read widely, an impression of the characteristics of the wines of various areas and districts will eventually be conveyed. A combination of reading, and visits (with tastings, of course) to wine areas is the best way of learning the salient characteristics. Chapter III should point the student in the right direction.

Over a period of time, one's memory will be usefully furnished with a library of names and tastes – together with the inevitable exceptions to the rules that ensure that one never has a dull moment.

──────────── *Deduction by bracketing* ────────────

To round off this section, here is a short exposition upon the useful method of bracketing, followed by two examples of the blind tasting technique. Bracketing also involves elimination. It is most useful when trying to assess the age of a wine.

Once again, some knowledge is required, this time of the vintage characteristics of the area one assumes, or knows, the wine to have come from.★ At one end of the bracket will be the oldest vintage it could possibly be; at the other the youngest. The bracket may extend over 10 or 20 years, or even longer in the case of really old wines.

The next stage is to jot down the most appropriate intervening vintages, eliminating the off-years if the wine is robust, well made and classic (and vice versa if the wine is light and feeble) until one is left with three or four possible vintage years. The final piece of elimination follows a thoughtful examination of the wine, comparing it against the known features of those singled-out vintages until, hopefully, one is left with just one inevitable choice of year. Incidentally, it is not sufficient merely to know that 1982, for example, was a big classic year in Bordeaux. It must also be borne in mind that not all the wines of the Bordelais are made in the same way, and that the types of grapes grown and blended can have different effects on the colour, bouquet and taste. One must know how the wines – at any rate the key wines – have developed in different districts, and be aware of the fact that the wines of St-Emilion, for example, and certain red graves, develop more quickly than the firmer wines of the Médoc. Once again, this sort of information is 'bracketed' in one's mind, and a conclusion often reached by the process of elimination described.

★Once again, readers are referred to *The Great Vintage Wine Book II* by Michael Broadbent (Mitchell Beazley, London, 1991), in which the salient characteristics of each vintage are described supported by tasting notes.

EXAMPLES

The trouble about trying to explain in words techniques that are second nature to the experienced taster is that the whole exercise is made to sound impossibly difficult. This is certainly not the intention. There is nothing I dislike more than the academic use of long words where short ones would do, as if one had to surround oneself with an off-putting protective layer of super-professionalism. My aim all along has been to try and break down the barriers of the unknown into logical and progressive steps. If words are used that sound curious and stultified (or even pure winemanship) to the layman, let him remember that every specialist has his own peculiar vocabulary, whether he be a musician, lawyer, gardener or judge of dogs at Cruft's.

To help explain how elimination techniques work in practice, here are two examples of wines tasted blind at a 1970★ Master of Wine study course. They were in a range of five unknown white and four unknown red wines. The approach and notes made were precisely as follows:

─────────── **'Wine No. 1' (red)** ───────────

Appearance Unusually deep, indicating hot vintage conditions, either naturally or of an abnormally hot summer and early autumn. In other words, from South Australia; or a big classic bordeaux of a particularly good year, or from the Rhône Valley. Just conceivably North African.

Actual colour a normal shade of red but with a marked purple edge to it, indicating immaturity.

A noticeably heavy bead ('legs') indicating high extract and glycerol. If, as is likely, the wine is from France, the combination of depth of colour and immature purple rules out poor vintages like '68 and '65. It is unlikely to be '67; more likely '66 and just possibly '64 if from the Médoc.

Bouquet 'Classic' and not 'foreign'. This rules out Australia, which often has a peculiar earthiness and hot burnt smell. The grape aroma, however, is not easy to identify; certainly not *cabernet*, *pinot* or *gamay*, which rules out Bordeaux, and Burgundy north and south.

It smells 'sweet', slightly scented, and certainly a heavyweight – the presence of considerable alcohol can be detected. Although young-looking there is an absence of raw, youthful, mouthwatering acidity on the nose.

By virtue of elimination, and the combination of great weight and lack of the usual raw acidity, one turns to the Rhône or possibly North Africa.

Palate Very slight sweetness for a red (i.e. not austerely dry like many a Médoc). As full-bodied as it looks: heavy in the mouth, revealing considerable weight of alcohol, and full of extract. Robust yet curiously soft (lacking the excess tannin and acidity of a bordeaux of the same weight and youthfulness). A nice, slightly scented flavour; still a little raw, and with a faintly bitter finish.

Conclusions A full-bodied, almost old-fashioned, Rhône wine from the south, around Châteauneuf. Good quality in its way; from an individual domaine, and of a big vintage, probably 1966.

(The wine was, in fact, Clos du Mont Olivet 1966. Estate-

★As the same principles still apply, I do not see much is gained by updating these examples.

bottled: Reflets du Châteauneuf-du-Pape. Alcoholic content over 14° G.L.)

────────────── **'Wine No. 2' (white)** ──────────────

Appearance Noticeably deeper than the other whites in the range. Deep, old-gold. Not very bright.

Distinctly an odd-man-out. From depth of colour could be a sweet dessert table wine or from some lesser region – perhaps Spain or southern Italy. Could also be due to considerable age in cask or bottle.

Bouquet Rich, honeyed. Clearly a dessert wine and although not very distinct, sufficiently classic to rule out Spain, Italy, etc. The honeyed overtones and richness would suggest *pourriture noble*, maturity and bottle-age. Probably a sweet bordeaux, or just possibly a sweet Loire like Coteaux du Layon.

Palate The sweetness confirmed: in fact a medium-sweet dessert wine. Medium-full bodied. Certainly sauternes (a sweet Loire would have had more acidity and less body).

Clean, straightforward, but with a rather short flavour which rules out first-growth quality but better than an ordinary sauternes supérieur. Balance quite good, indicating a soundly made wine of a fairly reasonable vintage with some maturity.

Conclusions A heavy barsac or medium sauternes of *bourgeois* quality, 1962 or 1964 vintage.

(The wine was Château Pajot 1964, London-bottled.)

────────────── **The ultimate test** ──────────────

After all this, it need hardly be restated that tasting blind – deducing a wine's precise origin and age – is the most severe test of a taster's true knowledge and ability.

Happily, however, it is not necessary to strive to reach, let alone to have reached, this stage of vinous ability in order to appreciate the taste of wine, and to enjoy drinking it. But if achievement in the higher realms of wine tasting *is* sought, it will now be apparent that a sensitive and trained palate alone is not enough: it has to be supported by real knowledge of areas and districts, of grape varieties, of styles and methods, and of vintage characteristics. And a good technique is helpful.

XI

FROM CELLAR
TO TABLE

Claret and Burgundy should be drank [sic] moderately warm. A
gentle warmth brings out an appreciation of body, diminishes the
astringency, and develops all the finer qualities prominently
including that of bouquet.
Arpad Haraszthy
Wines and Vines of California, 1889

The information in this chapter is a little off the subject of
tasting. Nevertheless, during the course of my travels – and
lectures – the question of decanting, airing time and temperatures (of storage and service) regularly arise. The following is,
therefore, a summary of my answers to these questions and I
hope that this practical advice will be found helpful.

CELLARS AND 'CELLARS'

There is no doubt about it, the traditional cold and slightly
damp cellar beneath the ground floor of the English and
Scottish country mansion was, and still is, ideal for the storage
of wine of all types.

But I, as an old-fashioned romantic, readily concede that an
above-ground, temperature and humidity controlled, wine
'cellar' will protect and preserve wine in the most demanding of
climates. During my frequent travels in the United States I have
witnessed the efficacy of airconditioning, the only problems
being the possible exposure to heat *en route* from supplier to
final destination, and failure of the electricity supply.

Temperature

Assuming that one has a single storage unit and wants to set the
air-conditioning unit at a steady year round temperature I
would suggest 55°F (13°C). This, in my experience, is the
average temperature of the traditional country house cellar. I
say average advisedly, for I have found it to vary from a fairly
rare, unvarying 48°F (9°C) – this was in the famous cellar at
Fasque, a house in Scotland belonging to the Gladstone family:
the whole house was cold; the cellar, a smallish, roughly seven
metres square, three-section cellar with stone floor, walls and
ceiling, beneath the centre rear of the house – to temperatures
well above 60°F (16°C) and even worse, those near to recently
installed boilers or with central heating pipes traversing the
cellar.

By and large, the best traditional cellars have been beneath the
ground floor but with air bricks or vents just above the outside
ground level. Ventilation is important, and a slight current of
air is considered essential to prevent stale air and muggy
conditions which encourage the formation of mould and rot.

I will just mention one remarkable modern cellar. Built in
California with three sections, the main area, in which cases of
youngish vintage wine are stacked, is maintained at a steady
55°F (13°C). Beyond it, through double glass doors is the old-
wine section where pre-phylloxera claret, ancient sauternes,
hock and other rarities are binned in metal racks at a
temperature of 50°F (10°C). The outer cellar area is held at 60°F
(16°C) or perhaps even a little warmer. Here are stored the very

young vintage ports, to encourage their development, and wines for everyday drinking.

Humidity

This is rarely a problem in country house cellars but is important to control in artificially maintained modern cellars. The ideal appears to be around 60%. Without adequate humidity there is the risk of corks drying out and shrinking.

The other extreme, damp, will not harm the wine but, if excessive, will soon cause labels to disintegrate, cartons to collapse and the base of wooden cases to rot. 'Bin-soiled' labels are not really worrying but become a problem when the labels become unreadable. The longer bottles are stored in a damp cellar the more the labels are likely to deteriorate, which is why vintage port was traditionally binned away unlabelled, identification being by means of bin labels, bottles having wax seals embossed with the vintage year and either the bottlers name or that of the shipper or his brand name. As the final line of defence, the long port corks are branded with the name of the port and its vintage.

The effect of a damp cellar can sometimes be catastrophic. I recently came across one in which a stack of cardboard wine cartons had collapsed and the contents, claret and burgundy of different châteaux, domaines and vintages, were very hard to sort out. Not only were the labels badly damaged but, to make matters worse, the weight of the collapsed boxes resulted in breakages which, in turn, stained the remaining labels.

For the unsophisticated I can define the ideal, which is based on Lord Rosebery's cellar at Dalmeny House, his Scottish seat. When entering the cellar there is a distinct chill: one needs warm clothing. And as for humidity, a gummed label will start to curl in seconds after it is put on a flat surface.

Shelves and bins

Without becoming too technical or complicated, the type of shelves or bins will depend partly on the space available and partly on the needs of the owner. Assuming that storage is to be as versatile as possible I recommend:

For long-term storage:
● an open space for stacking red bordeaux and any other wines in original wooden cases
● sturdy shelves one or two cases deep, one to three cases high, for storing cases and cartons. (One end of a box or carton usually bears the name of the wine. Keep this to the outer side)
● rectangular 'bins' or shelves two to four bottles deep, about 75 cm high and 90 cm wide, the bottles being stacked in rows on wooden laths. This is the traditional method and, for large quantities, is far and away the most economical use of space
● in diamond-shaped wooden wall bins, each side measuring roughly one metre. This is convenient for smallish quantitites.
For everyday use and small quantities:
● small bins or shelves, one bottle deep
● diamond-shaped bins as mentioned above
● traditional metal and wood single-bottle racks.
These are ideal for a collection of odd and old bottles but uneconomic in space for large runs of one wine.

Decanting table

It is handy to have a small table for making notes whilst binning, for decanting and for minor cellar equipment. I will not presume to enumerate such minutiae, save to say that many cellars I have been in, and not just in the United States, are incredibly elaborate with fancy lights, wall maps and a decoration of vinous miscellany.

──────── Bringing wine up from the cellar ────────

This is not meant to be superfluous waffle but practical advice. It is given in answer to questions I am frequently asked about how far in advance one brings up, or pulls out, wine for a dinner party, its temperature and how, in general, to handle it.

The need for looking ahead does not apply to ordinary wines, nor for most white wines. The following remarks apply to most good-quality red wines, claret in particular.

My practice is to bring the wine from the cellar at least 24 hours before the meal in question, standing the bottle upright on a sideboard in the dining room to give it reasonable time for the sediment to settle, also to allow the wine to lose its cellar chill and gradually attain room temperature. Never heat the bottle, either by standing it in front of a fire or in hot water.

Most restaurants have a 'dispense' area where a range of red wine is kept at drinking temperature. The selection is usually based on the more usually asked for wines, the rarer, more expensive bottles being stored at cellar temperature. So if you are planning a dinner party in a top-class restaurant with really good wine it is sensible to order the wines at least a day before to avoid the problem of having the red wine brought to the table too cold or, worse, 'just warmed a little, sir'.

──────── OPENING A BOTTLE ────────

When to draw the cork How far in advance should one open a bottle? This is a most frequently asked question, particularly in relation to fine and/or old wines, and one to which there is, paradoxically, no firm and sure answer. (The question does not arise for most white wines, rosés and the cheapest reds: just pull the cork and serve.)

If your vintage wine is old enough to have thrown a deposit then I recommend drawing the cork a couple of hours before decanting. The reason for this is that if there is a stubborn or difficult cork and one jolts the bottle and disturbs the sediment, the wine is given time to settle down again before decanting and serving. Leave the bottle upright after the cork is drawn and either balance the cork on the top or reinsert it fractionally.

Removing the cork This might not be deemed worthy of mention in a book on tasting but a great deal of ingenious thought, from the 18th century onwards, has been given to this essential operation.

The object of the exercise is to remove the cork cleanly, without it breaking or dropping bits into the wine, and without shaking the bottle and disturbing the sediment. Most corks give little trouble, and most corkscrews work, after a fashion.

However, some corkscrews are decidedly better than others. The best have added refinements such as ease of insertion and maximum pull for minimum effort. The early-to-mid-19th century patent continuous-action and ratchet types were undoubtedly the best★; the highly effective modern version is

★Those who would like to delve into this fascinating sideline are recommended to read the authoritative and well illustrated book on the subject, *Corkscrews for Collectors* by Bernard M. Watney and Homer D. Babbidge (Sotheby Parke Bernet, London and New York, 1981)

the Screwpull which for ease and ultimate refinement is outstandingly the most efficient, its only slight drawback being the time taken to remove the cork from the thread of the screw when drawn. As an added bonus, not thought of by the inventor, its base can be used as a candle holder. On occasion, the long corks of very old claret and of mature vintage port are best tackled with a long-shanked, broad-bladed corkscrew. Old claret corks can be crumbly and a broad-flanged corkscrew will give greater support, minimizing the bits of cork and cork powder dropping on to the surface of the wine. Some prefer compressed air cork removers; the cushion of air probably does not disturb the wine, but I have never liked the implement.

Vintage port poses a different problem. In addition to the length and strength of the cork, the traditional port bottle is slightly bulbous between the top of the shoulder and upper neck, the lower half of the cork swelling to form a very efficient air-excluding wedge which makes it difficult to extract the cork in one piece. In older bottles the applied glass top has an internal ridge which forms an obstruction. In face of these difficulties I normally partially insert the corkscrew and remove just the upper half of the cork, pushing the lower part back into the bottle. I find this is better than thrusting the corkscrew the full length of the cork and only pulling out bits.

On those rare occasions when the precise name and age of the port is unknown I break the bottle after decanting to retrieve the lower half of the cork and, matching it with the upper part previously removed, hope that branding will reveal the shipper's name and vintage year, an impossibility if a difficult cork has been removed in little pieces by just digging away with the corkscrew.

Cracking a bottle of port To 'crack a bottle' is an old colloquialism for opening/sharing a bottle. But if the bottle happens to be of old vintage port, the 'cracking' can be literal. One way is to use the back of a heavy knife, the other with port tongs. Both methods have as prime aim the literal cracking of the upper part of the neck in order to remove it cleanly, with the cork still in place. The top removed, one decants the port in the normal way. If necessary, one can then break the glass of the severed neck to remove the branded cork in one piece. I frequently do this to identify otherwise anonymous old bottles. It is sensible to wrap the neck in newspaper or an old cloth to stop fragments of glass flying around. I use a hammer, but with just sufficient force to crack the glass, not to damage the cork.

Now for the heavy blade and port tong techniques.

Perhaps I can best describe the first method by recalling a superb performance by an old friend, a retired colonel with an excellent cellar, who – quite unselfconsciously – at a great wine dinner held a bottle of old port in his left hand and, over the fireplace, with his right hand briskly swept the back of a sword upwards, more or less parallel with its neck. Catching the underside of the lip of the bottle he removed it, and the top of the neck, at one stroke. The bottle itself received a bit of a jolt but the crust was firmly formed and there was no problem decanting. Two words of advice: the back of a light modern bread knife will not do, an old fashioned carving knife is better – unless one has a cutlass handy. Also modern – say post 1960 – machine-made port bottles do not have a sharply jutting ledge just below the top of the neck like the bottles of old, which makes it difficult to hit it fair and square.

Port tongs are as traditional but, happily, in the right hands, more effective. The object is to introduce a sudden change of temperature which will crack the glass.

Take a pair of cast-iron port tongs (they can be bought from enterprising merchants of vinous artifacts) and stick the pincer end into the fire or on to a really hot stove until it is just about red hot. Clamp the tongs round the upper part of the neck of the bottle, hold them there for a few seconds to heat the glass then touch the neck with a cloth soaked in cold water. The neck will crack. Remove the whole of the top carefully so as not to disturb any shards of glass, and decant. The advantage of this method is that it works even with modern bottles.

—————— DECANTING ——————

More fatuous argument has been stimulated by this side issue than almost any other.

The reasons for decanting are quite elementary, and the procedure is not difficult.

The principal reason for decanting is to be in a position to serve wine clear and bright, leaving any bits of sediment in the bottom of the bottle instead of pouring it into the glasses. Does it matter? Well yes, it does. It is not only unsightly to have a hazy or bitty wine in the glass but the sediment, mainly dead colouring matter in red wine, will affect the taste.

The second, in my opinion far less important, reason for decanting is to aerate the wine. It is in this area that there is a great deal of muddled thinking so let me deal with this first.

————— Aerating wine or 'breathing time' —————

By general consensus, young wines can take, possibly need, plenty of breathing time, older wines less, very old wines scarcely any – just extract the cork and decant carefully.

If it were only as simple as that.

Once again I must preface my remarks by saying that the vast majority of the world's wines can be treated in an offhand way: just open and pour. Virtually all commercial reds, rosés and quite a few better quality whites do not change with exposure to air in normal serving and drinking conditions. However *all* will oxidize and 'flatten' in taste if left open or ullaged for any length of time, by which I mean several days.

So we are talking here about better class vintage wines, principally red.

The important thing to bear in mind is that once exposed to air, fine red wines will change. The main problem is to anticipate how much and how quickly.

The longer I deal with fine wines the more firmly convinced I am that if the wine is good – from a good vineyard, well made in a fine vintage year – when it is put into the bottle, then, as long as the storage conditions have been sound and the cork has not deteriorated, the wine will also be good, stable and drinkable when the cork is drawn, no matter what its age. A good sound wine – 5, 10, 25 or 50 years old – is unlikely to crack up shortly after the cork is extracted and the wine decanted; indeed quite the opposite, a century-old wine will catch its second breath, unfolding its bouquet, expanding and developing over a period of two or three hours, sometimes longer.

If the wine is of a poorish vintage and lacked body and balance when young, or if the storage has been poor, allowing the cork to shrink, then the wine is likely to break down very soon after it is poured out, in perhaps a matter of minutes.

Claret of a sturdy and more recent vintage, say a 1988 or a '86.

even one of the tougher '82s, will be so full of tannin and extract, so closed up, that decanting early afternoon for drinking around 8.30pm will encourage it to 'relax' and soften a little. How many times has one been told, and occasionally discovered accidentally, that a young red wine seems softer and better on the palate the next day? The same can occasionally happen to very old wine of the finest quality, though it is a brave or singularly curious man who will risk this.

It is my considered opinion that no noticeable oxidation occurs for a very considerable period after the cork is drawn, and, surprisingly, little change occurs in the decanter. The main development takes place in the glass. The greater the wine, the more revealing and complex the bouquet and the longer it and the flavour will last. To give an example: at a recent Bordeaux Club dinner my reds opened with a (my only) bottle of Lafite 1961. The problem was how to present this wine at its very best. I took the wine from my London cellar to Christie's cellar two weeks in advance. The day before the dinner I brought it carefully up to my office, leaving it standing upright. The afternoon of the dinner, I dusted the bottle gently, removed the capsule and wiped the top, first with a damp cloth then with clean dry kitchen paper. The cork was drawn about 5pm and stood loose on the top, less to prevent air than dust from getting in. The wine was decanted at 6.45pm into a rather wide-mouthed carafe, without a stopper, and carried at 7.30, just before the first guest arrived, to the boardroom where we were to have dinner. It was actually served at 8.30pm. By 9pm the bouquet had blossomed nicely and by 9.45 it had developed fully, with a nice warm, spicy, biscuity fragrance. I kept a little in my glass and two hours after it had first been poured it still smelled incredibly delicious. As a matter of interest, the last of four red wines I served was an 1875 Château Desmirail. The bottle had an excellent provenance. It came from the private cellar in Paris of a noted connoisseur, had been recorked, probably in the mid 1930s, and its level was still good. In the middle of the dinner I returned to my office to draw the cork and decant the wine which was then served right away. To describe this remarkable pre-phylloxera claret would need another chapter. Suffice to say that there was not a trace of decay on nose or palate. It seemed fatter and rounder after 15 minutes and even an hour later, the scent in the emptied glass was exquisite.

My final advice on 'air' is: be bold, and try decanting well in advance. Above all, with a really fine wine (and this applies as much to a top-class white burgundy as to claret) give the wine a chance to blossom in the glass: sip it, make it last, revel in its marvellous development.

Why decant?

Before recommending the best method of decanting let me again mention those wines which rarely if ever, need decanting. Basically, they are all wines without a sediment: very young red wines, ordinary commercial red table wines, young white wines, including sherry, also rosés, champagne, ruby and tawny wood ports and less expensive madeira.

White wines that benefit from decanting are old ones, whether sweet or dry, which quite frequently have a slight powdery sediment, sometimes younger whites which, through a sudden change of temperature, have a tartrate deposit — perfectly harmless and tasteless white crystals — and some rare old sherries and old solera and vintage madeiras. The latter, with their glowing amber colours, and old sauternes, usually a beautiful warm yellow-orange, shot with gold highlights, look particularly beautiful in clear glass or cut glass decanters.

Prime candidates for decanting are mature claret and vintage port. Even young claret, which has had little time to throw a sediment, might as well be decanted. It does give the wine a little air which has a slight softening effect and, in any case, the colour always looks so attractive.

When it comes to red burgundy, there are two schools of thought. In Burgundy itself, the wine is rarely decanted. I am not at all sure of the reason for this, but I *am* sure that great care must be taken when pouring from the bottle and ample time given for the sediment to settle. You need a steady hand or an old-fashioned decanting cradle with a cranking handle and smooth action. In the latter instance, the glasses are brought to the decanting cradle, not cradle to glasses. If this contraption is not used, for most of us do not possess one, then I recommend that the glasses are all lined up alongside the bottle, the wine being poured steadily into each glass. In either case, it is essential for the pouring to stop before the sediment reaches the upper neck. (I recently witnessed a magnum of beautiful burgundy being spoiled by my host, a noted connoisseur, who poured steadily into eight large glasses, continuing round to the bitter end, giving everyone's glass a final *coup de grâce* of sediment!) I personally consider that mature red burgundy should be decanted. It is far safer.

--------------------- **Method** ---------------------

The bottle must have been left resting, preferably upright, undisturbed for an hour or two, better still, for a day, before decanting so that the sediment has had time to settle. This is, of course, particularly vital if, as I recommend, the bottle has been moved from cellar or store to the dining room, or wherever one decides to decant. The only exceptions are, perhaps, old sauternes which are intended to be served cold and can be decanted in the cellar, and vintage port which can be lifted carefully from the bin and decanted on the spot.

So, assuming that the bottle of claret or burgundy has been standing upright, capsule removed and cork extracted, the following should be ready at hand:

Decanter Clean, dry, sweet smelling and also at room temperature. (It is amazing how little thought is given to the temperature of the decanter and glasses. There is no point, having nursed the wine to room temperature, in putting it into decanters and glasses which have been removed at the last minute from a cold cupboard.) Incidentally, if the stopper has been left in a decanter for any length of time the air within can smell stale, particularly if the decanter had not been properly rinsed out and left upside down to dry before it was put away.

Candle For me, the ideal is a four to six inch candle in a table top candle holder. The base of a Screwpull corkscrew works admirably. A tall tapering candle in an equally tall candle stick is impossible to decant over unless it is on a low table or stool.

The alternative to a candle, and as effective, is an electric light bulb or torch placed on the table top and shining upwards.

Funnel A plain glass funnel is best. A plastic funnel looks nasty and I always worry about its cleanliness. Silver funnels look splendid, but when and with what were they last cleaned? Traces of metal polish will taint the wine.

There is just one type of wine for which I personally use a funnel and sieve, and that is for vintage port. The reason for this is that the sediment of vintage port, known as the crust, is heavy and flaky. The wine pours bright and one merely catches the crust in the sieve.

Procedure

Place the cradle holder on the edge of a table top, the decanter to the left, the bottle to the right – unless you happen to be left-handed.

Make sure that the neck, shoulder and at least the upper half of the bottle is free of cellar dust or grime which will otherwise obscure the view through the glass.

If you have a funnel, put it into the neck of the decanter. If not, and a funnel is not absolutely essential, one just has to pour slowly and carefully.

Now either leave the decanter where it is or pick it up by the neck with the left hand – all depends on you, and the height of the candle, the flame of which should be about four inches below the level of the top of the funnel.

Place the right hand over the lower half of the bottle, not at the upper or shoulder end, pick it up and tip it gently over the rim of the funnel or the lip of the decanter. Start pouring slowly but steadily. Once the wine has started flowing then manoeuvre the bottle gently towards the lighted candle so that the eye, the underside of the shoulder of the bottle and the candle are in a straight line. Do not line up vertically, i.e. with the bottle directly above the candle, as the flame from the candle will smoke up the glass and obscure one's view of the wine. A slight angle is better. Do not stop pouring whilst this manoeuvring is going on otherwise the sediment might be disturbed.

By the time you have reached the right position, a little over half the contents will have been poured and the wine should be showing clear and bright as it passes over the shoulder into the neck. Continue pouring steadily, watching carefully for the first traces of light powdery sediment which will be easing up the underside of the bottle. I personally let the very light sediment move up, and if a fair amount of wine is still in the bottle, continue until the main swirl of heavier sediment appears. Let this slide across the shoulder of the bottle but do *not* let it enter the neck. This is the moment to stop. By now the base of the bottle will be higher than the neck. To stop decanting, quickly but smoothly swing the base down. It is more effective than pulling the bottle away horizontally from the funnel as this movement results in the remaining wine welling into the neck, risking sediment spilling into the decanter.

The amount and type of sediment will vary to some extent depending on the style and age of the wine, but the method described above should cope with all situations. Burgundy bottles have more gently sloping shoulders and one has to be a little more careful than with bordeaux or bordeaux-style bottles which have rounded corners to delay the sediment.

Vintage port The bottles used traditionally by English merchants to bottle port were of extremely dark glass, often so dark that the level of the wine cannot be seen even if the bottle is held against a high-powered spotlight.

The sediment or crust is also different. This forms along the lower side of the bottle. It is a continuous process. The sooner a vintage port is laid down (binned) after bottling and the longer it is left undisturbed the more steadily and firmly the crust will form, and, as a result, the easier it will be to decant when it is fully mature.

With an old (say 25 years or older) vintage port no candle is needed when decanting. Traditionally port used to be decanted in the cellar: the bottle would be lifted gently from the bin, put into a wooden cradle (not a flimsy basketwork version), the cork extracted and the wine poured steadily into the decanter via a funnel with a sieve. The wine would inevitably be bright, its black, flaky, filmy crust being caught by the sieve.

Muslin and filter papers The use of a strainer is very tempting. It appeals to the timid, the palsied handed and, dare I say it, the mean-minded amongst us.

Frankly, if the wine has been handled properly, cellared for a decent length of time, brought from cellar to sideboard to settle and uncorked properly there should be no need to use a filter.

On the other hand, even the most farsighted and careful will on occasion find themselves with a rush job or inadvertently to have disturbed the bottle, giving the wine insufficient time to settle down. This is perhaps the only good excuse for using a piece of fine clean muslin or linen cloth over the funnel to act as a filter. Filter pads – those used for coffee – are a fairly untenable last resort. My own experience is that muslin rarely does a proper job and filter pads can give the wine a slightly powdery taste and can even take the stuffing out of a wine.

As for extracting the last ounce of liquid from a bottle by filtering the remnants, sediment and all, this, in my opinion, is shortsighted. The dregs, however well strained, do not taste good, and if tippped into the decanter slightly spoil the rest of the otherwise bright and sound wine.

Cloudy wine One occasionally comes across a bottle of wine which has a suspended haze of very fine particles which will not settle. If it has been recently purchased from the regular supplier take it back. If it is a very old wine there is little one can do. It is probably worth trying a filter pad, but the wine might not be up to much anyway.

Glasses Another word on the subject of glasses. The 'ideal' tasting glass is illustrated on page 49. As it happens this is a most excellent size and shape for virtually all white and red wines. However, a table setting looks more interesting if one uses different glasses for different types of wine. I personally like a slightly smaller tulip-shaped glass for my white wine and matching, but larger, glasses for reds. Having for years scorned 'gold-fish bowls' I must confess a liking for fairly large rounded glasses for burgundy: the perfume seems to arise more exotically from them. But do remember that large glasses use up a lot of wine and, a minor phenomenon, the larger the glasses the more one's guests drink (if you do not believe this, do a little experimenting).

Dessert wines and vintage ports are often served in small glasses, which is a mistake. A medium-sized tulip or thistle glass is better than a copita, ghastly schooner or thimble.

In addition to shops specializing in glasses, many wine merchants now carry a range, sometimes uniquely their own.

— THE TEMPERATURE OF WINES AT TABLE —

It may be comforting, or irritating, to be told that there is no such thing as a precise temperature at which a specific wine should be served. The season of the year and the temperature of the dining room itself have a bearing. One thing is certain, extremes are undesirable. Having said this, the temperature of wine *is* important and lack of consideration will result in a wine performing less well than it should.

Red wines

It is said that red wines should be served at room temperature. This is a broad generality, for not only are some dining rooms too cold and some too hot, but the age and weight of red wines require different serving temperatures.

● Young red bordeaux tends to have a high level of tannin and a certain raw austerity. The bigger the wine and the younger the vintage, the warmer it should be served: say 65°F (18°C), even up to 68°F (20°C) in a warm room or on a warm day

● Mature red bordeaux: about 65°F (18°C). On a hot June day in 1970 I well remember a fine claret (it was a 15-year-old Domaine de Chevalier) being served at a Master of Wine lunch. The temperature seemed perfect. To my surprise, when tested with a thermometer it turned out to be 70°F (21°C)

● Old red bordeaux (of the vintage 1964 and older) should not be served too warm. It seems to take the stuffing out of the wine. Possibly a maximum of 63°F (17°C) depending on the natural room temperature

● Red burgundy. A good burgundy should definitely be served cooler than claret. In Burgundy itself it is very often brought straight from the cellar. Burgundy is less tannic, usually more alcoholic and slightly sweeter. It tastes livelier if served around 60°F (16°C)

● Rhône and other full-bodied reds: about 60°F (16°C) or, if very tannic, up to 68°F (20°C)

● Beaujolais and red wines from the Loire: serve cool, say between 54°–58°F (12°–15°C)

White wines

It is generally true to say that white wines should be served cold. But how cold? In my experience, far more care is needed to get the temperature right for white than for red. I shall just deal with recommended temperatures, then with the methods of achieving and holding those levels.

● Light dry acidic wines: Muscadet and the range of light, refreshing wines made with the *sauvignon blanc* grape such as Sancerre should be served cold, between 45°–50°F (7°–10°C)

● Fine white burgundy: I single this out for special treatment for though it is always dry, the alcoholic content can be surprisingly high, in the 12.8% to 14% range. It is therefore a big mistake to serve, say, a Bâtard-Montrachet too cold. I would suggest 30 minutes in the refrigerator and let it rise almost to room temperature in the glass. The bouquet will develop miraculously.

● Medium-dry German wines and others with a light fruity-acid balance: about 48°–50°F (9°–10°C)

● Sweet white wines: the finer the wine the less cold it should be served. A minor sauternes-type wine and any sweet wine low in acidity should be served very cold, near to 45°F (7°C). A top class mature sauternes not less than 50°F (10°C).

Chilling white wines The late Otto Loeb drank *Trockenbeerenauslesen* poured at room temperature into ice-cold glasses. I tried this recently. It seemed to work but the glasses did not stay cold long.

To chill a standard-size bottle of white wine in an average refrigerator set at say 42°F (5°C) will take roughly 30 minutes to reach 59°F (15°C), and 1 hour to reach 55°F (13°C). In 2 hours it will have dropped below 50°F (10°C).

The problem with white wine is keeping it at the prescribed serving temperatures. Old fashioned ice buckets are, in my opinion, unsatisfactory. In them wine tends to become over chilled. Moreover, they are messy to use and labels come off. So I should recommend using ice buckets only for light dry white or sparkling wines which can endure maximum chilling. A practical tip: do not use chips or cubes of ice alone; instead part fill the bucket with water so that the bottle can be put back into the bucket easily. A generous sprinking of salt keeps the temperature down.

The ideal way to keep white wine at an even serving temperature after chilling is to stand the bottle in a Vinicool®★ open-topped flask. The bottle will hold its temperature for the entire time needed for serving and drinking. Vinicool® vacuum flasks are used regularly at pre-sale tastings at Christie's: they have the added advantage of being transparent so one can see the labels on the bottles.

Glasses for white wines are, conventionally, smaller than for red. The reason for this is largely ignored, or taken for granted: there is a smaller surface area of wine and glass to transmit the warmth of the room. My last tip is to pour only a half-glass at a time, topping up frequently from the cool bottle.

Rosés

Pink wine from whatever source, serve cold: 45°–50°F (7°–10°C).

Champagne

Cheap nonvintage champagne and sparkling wines, serve very cold. However, the bouquet and flavour of fine vintage champagne, like great white burgundy, is muted and suppressed if served too cold. Serve cool enough to be refreshing but not so cold that the glasses become frosted.

Sherry

Serve cheaper sherry and sherry-type wines cold. Fine finos and manzanillas are more refreshing slightly chilled, say around 48°F (9°C). Serve fine old amontillados and olorosos at room temperature. It is sometimes suggested that 'cream' sherry should be served on the rocks: so be it!

Madeira

Temperature depends on the grape style:
● Sercial, the lightest and driest, serve cool, say 48°–50°F (9°–10°C)
● Verdelho, roughly medium dry, also cool but not too cold
● Bual, richer and fuller bodied, I suggest around 55°F (13°C) or, if old and fine, over 60°F (16°C)
● Malmsey, the sweetest and richest, at room temperature

Port

A surprising variation of temperatures is recommended:
● White port is generally dry or medium-dry so serve very cold
● Ordinary ruby or tawny is generally drunk at room or 'pub' temperature
● Fine old tawny is the favourite drink of the port shippers in Oporto where they serve it cool
● Vintage port at room temperature

★Obtainable from some wine merchants and speciality stores.

XII

FULL GLOSSARY
OF TASTING TERMS

*The first difficulty that tasters encounter is to find and
to translate into precise and clear language the qualities and
defects of a wine . . .*
Pierre Bréjoux
Revue du Vin de France, 1977

acetic vinegary smell; sharp, over-tart on the palate. A vinegary condition resulting from the action of acetobacter, harmful ferments that attack wine left open in bottle, or fermented at too high a temperature, or carelessly bottled. Ullaged wine, whether in cask or bottle, will usually be suspect. The latter is usually due to poor, wormy or dried-out corks, which let air in and wine out (weepers), the remaining wine often becoming acetic and undrinkable.

acetone a high-toned estery aroma connected with the ester ethyl acetate or with nail-varnish-like amyl acetate.

acid, acidity on the nose: mouth-watering, refreshing (tartaric), sometimes like raw cooking apples (malic); detectable on the tongue, giving wine essential crispness and zing. 'Volatile' acids are more pronounced on the nose, 'fixed' acids (tartaric, succinic and citric) less so. Esters of both acids make an important contribution to the overall bouquet of wine. There are several types and degrees of acidity commonly found in wine, some beneficial and some detrimental. The right sort of natural acidity is an essential component of a sound wine; it acts as a preservative, produces bouquet and provides the essential bite and finish. It also stimulates the gastric juices – one of the oft-forgotten main purposes of any table wine. Lack of acidity can be detected by a general flabbiness, lack of vitality and a weak watery finish; excess acidity by a sharp tart effect on the tongue. Youthful acidity tends to mellow with age. Some wines, such as vinho verde, champagne and wines from the Saar and Ruwer, have a deliberately and refreshingly high acid content. Fruity-acidity is perhaps the most desired characteristic of German wines (*see also* TARTARIC, MALIC and SORBIC ACIDS).

aftertaste the internal bouquet that sometimes remains in the throat and back nasal passages after a wine has been drunk. Unpleasant if the wine is strong-flavoured and in poor condition; at its best, however, the hallmark of a great wine and usually part of what is more poetically referred to as a lingering farewell.

aggressive more than lively on the palate, perhaps over tannic.

alcohol an essential component, binding and preserving. In *pure* form the higher alcohols, amyl and butyl, have an unpleasant, throat-catching odour, phenethyl has an intense, rose-like smell and ethanol a burning sensation. However, diluted, as in wine, alcohol is scarcely detectable on the nose, though it can be assessed by its weight in the mouth, by a sort of burning taste and cumulatively, by its well-known effects on the head of the imbiber. Alcohol has a certain sweetness, giving richness and warmth to full-bodied wines. Although table wines may vary by only 3° (3% by volume), from light mosels around 11° to Rhône and sauternes in the 13° to 14° bracket, the effect on the weight, character and strength of the wine is marked.

almonds, bitter the smell of almond kernels or bitter almonds emanates from a badly fined wine, possibly, but rarely, after using illegal 'blue' fining. Probably drinkable but not sound.

apples a fresh, raw smell, indicative of an immature young wine (*see* MALIC ACID). Tokay has an old apple scent.

aroma that part of the smell of wine derived from the grape, whether distinctly varietal or merely vinous (oenologists also use the word in respect of odours resulting from fermentation), as opposed to 'bouquet' which is derived from the development of the wine itself in bottle.

aromatic fragrant, a richness of aroma and taste, spicy overtones, particularly from aromatic grape varieties, such as *muscat*.

asbestos odour imparted by new filter pads or old, dirty, overused pads in bottling. Wine has flat, alkaline taste. Asbestos is harmless if ingested.

astringent a dry, mouth-puckering effect caused by a high tannin content (often accompanied by a high degree of acidity). Might well soften and mellow as the wine matures. Not bitter.

attenuated becoming thin on the palate, losing fruit and flesh, usually in respect of an old wine.

austere somewhat tough and severe; simple, uncomplex, possibly undeveloped.

backward retarded, undeveloped for its age/vintage.

baked a 'hot' rather earthy smell produced by burnt and shrivelled grapes due to excessive sunshine and lack of rainfall. A characteristic of red wine produced in hot vintages in the Rhône valley and in naturally hot wine-producing areas such as southern California, Australia and South Africa.

balance the combination and relationship of components (*see* WELL BALANCED).

banana overtone on the bouquet of wines made from frost-bitten grapes; also a specific smell of old wine in poor condition.

beefy substantial, muscular, well endowed with alcohol, tannic, extract.

beery an undesirable smell and taste caused by secondary fermentation in bottle. The wine may be drinkable, just, but will be basically unsound, poor on finish.

beetroot, boiled reminiscent of, and recognition symbol for, the *pinot noir* grape aroma.

big manly wine, well-endowed with vital elements, not just high in alcohol.

bite implying a substantial degree of acidity (plus tannin). A good factor in young wine. Generally mellows with age.

bitter, bitterness detected on the palate, on the back of the tongue and finish. Mainly unpleasant. A taste, not a tactile sensation, though it can be a desirable quality in certain wines (usually an acquired taste) and vermouths. Bitterness is derived from either chemical salts or vegetable extracts. A certain bitterness can be imparted by colouring matter, though the depositing of this during maturation will normally reduce its pristine harshness. Polyphenols extracted from wooden casks, particularly when dirty and contaminated, will also, when oxidized, impart a bitter taste. More rarely an unpleasant bitterness is due to *amertume*, a bacteriological disease.

bitters substances added to wine (for example, in the making of vermouth) that have a bitter taste and stimulate the appetite and digestion. They can be of vegetable origin, like gentian, or aromatic, containing volatile oil, like orange peel. Quinine has a similar effect, plus additional properties such as a remote action on the nervous system.

blackcurrants the nearest fruit-smell to the *cabernet sauvignon* grape. Detectable to some degree wherever the grape is used but particularly marked on wines from Pauillac, and to a slightly lesser extent Margaux. Perhaps the first major clue to red bordeaux wine in a blind tasting.

bland not complimentary: mild, easy, characterless; but not unpleasant.

body the weight of wine in the mouth due to its alcoholic content, extract and to its other physical components. These factors stem from the quality of the vintage and geographical origin, and in turn affect the style and quality of the wine. Wines from hotter climates tend to have more body than those from the north (compare the Rhône with the Mosel, for example).

botrytis short for *botrytis cinerea* known also as noble rot, *pourriture noble*, *edelfäule*: the phenomenal rot which is encouraged to develop on the skins of grapes in Sauternes and the best vineyards in Germany during the delayed autumn harvest. Botrytis shrivels the grapes, reduces the water content and concentrates the sugar. The effect on nose and palate is akin to honey.

bottle-age extremely hard to describe but easily recognizable on the bouquet to an experienced taster and a vital factor in the judgment of a wine's age/maturity and development in bottle. On white dessert wines a mellow, honeyed quality; on reds a breaking down of raw edges to reveal fully evolved character, softness and mellowness.

bottle-sickness temporary oxidation after bottling.

bottle stink stale air smell on drawing the cork, usually wears off quickly.

bouquet in the broadest and most often-used sense, the pleasant and characteristic smell of wine. In the narrower sense, the odour created by the wine's own development: by the esters and aldehydes formed by the slow oxidation of fruit acids and alcohol (*see also* AROMA).

breed finesse arising out of the pedigree of a wine.

buttery self-descriptive smell and taste (not texture).

caramel a slightly burnt, toffee-like flavour which can have a literal origin in the case of certain spirits but can only be reminiscent in the case of wine. A characteristic flavour of madeira and marsala, for example.

carbon dioxide responsible for the sparkle of champagne and sparkling wines, also the tingle of *spritzig* or slightly effervescent *pétillant* table wines.

cats the smell of tom cats, a strangely attractive grape smell associated with certain young white wines.

cat's piss an inelegant but appropriate description of the aroma of an acidic *sauvignon blanc*.

cedarwood characteristic scent of many fine clarets.

chaptalization or addition of sugar to must, increases strength, softens tannins and improves unripe acid grapes in a poor vintage.

character a wine of any quality which has unmistakable and distinctive features.

characteristic having the style and character of the grape, district, vintage, etc. Often sweepingly used to avoid a detailed description.

chocolaty a chocolate-like smell and taste, rich, thick, slightly vanilla. Not bad, not unusual (some burgundies), but inelegant and not a pure varietal characteristic.

cidery smell, a defect, early oxidation.

cinnamon taste of immature wine made in new oak casks.

clean absence of foreign and unpleasant odour and taste.

cloying a sweet and heavy wine which palls; lacking the acidity to make it crisp and interesting.

coarse rough texture; lacking breed and possibly indifferently made. Do not confuse coarseness with the rough rawness of a fine but completely immature wine.

common lacking breed, but none the less sound and drinkable.

complex many-faceted smell and taste. The hallmark of a well developed fine wine.

cooked a heavy, sometimes sweet but not unpleasant smell from the use of sugar, concentrated grape juice or high temperature during vinification.

corked an off, oxidized and thoroughly obnoxious smell. An overused and misunderstood expression; the *sommelier's* scourge.

corky having a distinct smell of cork, arising from a poor, soft or disintegrating cork, or one infected by weevil. A poor cork can, of course, let air in, in which case the wine may oxidize completely and become corked. The two expressions are frequently interchanged due to lack of agreement over definition.

creaming or crémant a light, slightly frothy *mousse*. Half-sparkling.

crisp a desirable feature in white wines; firm, refreshing, with positive acidity.

cruising mid-red colour, neither immature nor fully mature.

deep an adjective that needs qualification: deep-coloured; deep bouquet, depth of flavour – opposite to superficial; indicating underlying richness, layers of flavour.

delicate charm and balance in a light wine of some quality.

depth richness, subtlety – seemingly 'layers' of flavour, all interlocked and supportive.

developed in relation to wine is a stage of maturity: undeveloped, well-developed (mature, balanced, rounded), overdeveloped (overmature, cracking up).

distinguished notable character and breed.

dry not sweet; absence of residual sugar; fully fermented.

dull appearance not bright; nose and palate lacking interest and zest.

dumb undeveloped, but with inherent promise of quality. Often the sign of an adolescent stage.

dusty an evocative cellar-like smell; possibly high tannic content – or dirty glasses.

earthy characteristic overtone derived from certain soils.

eggs, bad (hydrogen sulphide) disagreeable, but harmless. Probably due to bad cellar treatment.

elegant stylish balance and refined quality.

estery high-toned, acetone smell. An ester results from the reaction of an organic acid and alcohol.

eucalyptus descriptive, analogous, spicy bouquet associated with certain top-quality *cabernet sauvignon*, notably Heitz Martha's Vineyard which is surrounded by eucalyptus trees which probably do affect the grapes, but also some of the finest ripe vintages of Château Latour.

extract soluble solids (strictly speaking excluding sugar) which add to a wine's body and substance.

farmyard a ripe, earthy, manure-like, sometimes pigsty smell probably due to the presence of butyric acid, one of the several normal volatile acids which, in excess, creates the smell described. Not uncommon in even major classified red bordeaux.

fat fullish body, high in glycerol and extract. If sweet, verging on unctuous.

feminine subjective and abstract term indicating a style of wine which is attractive, not heavy or severe, with charm – delightful qualities that all but a misogynist might conjure up!

filter-pads *see* ASBESTOS.

fine an all-embracing expression of superior quality. Perhaps the most overworked adjective in the vinous vocabulary.

finesse grace, delicacy, distinction.

finish the end-taste. A wine cannot be considered well balanced without a good finish, by which is understood a firm, crisp and distinctive end. The opposite, a short or poor finish, will be watery, the flavour not sustained and tailing-off inconclusively. The correct degree of the right sort of acidity is a decisive factor.

firm implies a sound constitution and balance, positive in the mouth, as opposed to flabby.

flabby feeble, lacking crisp acidity, probably without finish. Either a poor wine or one that is cracking up.

flat dull, insipid, lacking acidity. Or merely a sparkling wine which has lost its sparkle.

flinty an evocative overtone. Certain white-wine grapes grown on certain soils have a hint of gunflint in the bouquet and flavour, e.g. Pouilly *blanc-fumé*.

flowery fragrant, flower-like. Certain mosels in full bloom.

forceful strong, assertive character, probably well endowed with tannin and acidity.

forward advanced in maturity for its age or vintage.

foxy the curious and distinctive earthy tang, flavour and finish of wine made from native American vine species. It does not imply an animal smell but relates to the wild or 'fox' grapes.

fragrant attractively and naturally scented.

fresh retaining natural youthful charm, vitality (and acidity).

fruity attractive, fleshy quality derived from good ripe grapes; but not necessarily a grapey aroma.

full (bodied) high in alcoholic content and extract. Filling the mouth. A table wine with an alcoholic content probably over 13° G.L. (Gay Lussac, i.e. percentage of alcohol by volume). In the context of fortified wines a heavy sherry, port or madeira at the top of the alcohol and sugar scale.

gamey overripe, touch of decay, often on the verge of cracking up. As with game birds, very old burgundy and claret can be attractive, if something of an acquired taste.

garlic, wild a faint reminiscent whiff denoting the presence of sorbic acid.

gentle mild, pleasant, unassertive.

geraniums not a complimentary flower simile: a geranium-like odour caused by the presence of an obscure micro-organism derived principally from esters formed during fermentation.

goaty a rich ripe animal-like flavour. For example, ripe fat Pfalz wines made from the *traminer* grape.

graceful abstract term: elegant, stylish.

grapey a rich muscat-like aroma produced by certain grape varieties, including *muscatelle* and crossings like *scheurebe* and *Müller-Thurgau*.

great almost as overworked as fine. Should be confined to wines of the highest quality which, in practice, means top growths of good years: having depth, richness, character, style, complexity, fragrance, length and aftertaste.

green unripe, raw and young. Youthful, mouth-watering acidity produced by immature grapes, or the unsettled acidity of an immature wine.

grip a firm and emphatic combination of physical characteristics. A desirable quality in port, for example. The opposite to flabbiness and spinelessness.

gritty coarse-textured in the mouth.

hard severity due to the overprominence of tannin and, to a lesser extent, acidity. Usually the product of a hot vintage or overprolonged contact with skins and pips during fermentation. Time usually mellows.

harsh self-descriptive. Due to excess tannin and/or ethyl acetate associated with acetic acid.

heady high in alcohol. Tipsy-making.

hearty robust, zestful, warm, alcoholic; generally in respect of red wine.

heavy more than just full-bodied; overendowed with alcohol and extract. Watch out for the context in which it is used. For example, a strapping Rhône wine will appear too heavy for a light summer luncheon but would be the right weight to accompany a steak and kidney pie in midwinter. 'Heavy' is also an official definition: a fortified wine subject to the higher rates of duty.

hedonistic a simple, subjective, personal rating.

herbaceous between grasslike and flowery. Pleasant, open, fresh, appealing. Usually young white wines.

high-toned nose of assertive volatile character.

hollow a wine with a foretaste and some finish but without sustaining middle-flavour. A failing rather than a fault.

honest a somewhat condescending term for a decent, well-made but fairly ordinary wine; true to type.

honeyed characteristic fragrance of certain fine mature wines such as sauternes and *Beerenauslesen*; also indicative of bottle-age.

implicitly sweet apparent sweetness from sources other than sugar, e.g. glycerol, alcohol.

inky 'red ink': an unpleasant, tinny, metallic taste due to the presence of tannate of iron produced by the action of tannin on iron – a nail in a cask will have this effect. (Tannate of iron is the chief constituent of ink.)

insipid flat, somewhat tasteless. Lacking firmness, character.

iron a faintly metallic, earthy-iron taste derived from the soil. Noticeable in some St-Emilions and in these circumstances entirely natural, adding recognizable character.

lanolin a soft, sweet harmonious, possibly slightly oily smell like lanolin, associated with classic wines made from the *chenin blanc* and *sémillon* grapes in good years.

leathery reds rich in tannin (leather is made by hides or skins being impregnated with tannin).

legs the English term for globules which drip or ooze down the sides of the glass after the wine is swirled. Also known as 'tears'. Generally indicative of a rich wine (*see also* p. 54).

lemon lemon-like overtones. For example, noticeable on some fine but immature white Hermitage wines.

length the longer the flavour the finer the wine. The French use the word persistence and measure it in seconds.

light a low degree of alcohol (under 12° G.L.). Lack of body. A desirable characteristic of certain styles of wine like young beaujolais and Mosel-Saar-Ruwer wines. Rather confusingly, 'light' is an official term for a natural, unfortified table wine.

limpid clear, luminous (appearance).

limpidity colour appears to have extra sheen, outstanding brightness, luminosity.

little scarcely any bouquet or aroma. Either a wine of no quality or character, or dumb. A minor wine.

lively fairly explicit. Usually in reference to a fresh, youthful wine; or an old wine with fresh and youthful characteristics.

long length of flavour in mouth; a sign of quality.

luscious soft, sweet, fat, fruity and ripe. All these qualities in balance.

macération carbonique a 'whole-fruit' modern method of wine-making involving the fermentation of the whole grape. The results are, at best, a pleasant, fresh, quaffable style of wine; at worst, tinny. The author's view is that this method reduces the individual character of wines, those of one district tasting much like another.

maderized the heavy flat smell of an overmature, somewhat oxidized white wine (sometimes accompanied by brown-tinged colour and flat taste). *See also* OXIDIZED.

malic acid although without merit, its presence due to unripe 'green' grapes has mouthwatering, cooking-apple effect; mouth-puckering. A 'malolactic' fermentation in cask converts the raw malic acid into softer and more amenable lactic acid.

manly or masculine: positive, possibly assertive, even aggressive; a big wine, muscular.

mature the maturity of a wine is one of its most crucial factors. Wines vary enormously in make-up and take anything from a matter of months to many years to reach full maturity, depending mainly on their tannin, acid and alcohol content. Maturity can be detected on nose and palate; the maturity of red wines is most easily and visibly measured by the brownness of the rim. An immature wine has raw, unknit, component parts. A perfectly mature wine has all its constituent elements in harmony.

mawkish a trifle flat, drab-flavoured, sickly.

meaty heavy, rich almost chewable quality, mellow yet tannic.

medium (body) neither light nor heavy in alcohol and extract – probably between 12° and 13° G.L., depending on the style of wine.

medium-dry containing some residual sugar but dry enough to be drunk before or during a meal.

medium-sweet considerable residual sugar, but not really a dessert wine. Many German wines come into this category and are better drunk alone, without food.

mellow soft, mature. No rough edges. A desirable characteristic normally associated with maturity and age; also essentially associated with alcohol, glycerol and fructose.

mercaptan a slightly sour, unpleasant, rubbery smell indicating deterioration, in some old hock, for example, due to the breakdown of sulphur dioxide, originally used as a preservative.

metallic tinny – not a pleasant quality (*see also* INKY). Usually due to some metallic contamination during wine-making, storage in cask or bottling. If distinctly unpleasant and associated with a deepening of colour (of white wine) and a tawny deposit, it is usually due to copper contamination.

mouldy an undesirable flavour imparted by rotten grapes or stale, unclean casks, etc.

mousey smell and taste, flat yet acetic. Sign of bacteriological disease, *tourne*, usually affecting only wine in cask.

mulberry a more opulent, succulent type of fruitiness, softer than the blackcurrant of young *cabernet sauvignon*, associated with exceptional ripe claret, often with *merlot* dominating.

mushrooms fresh picked. A pleasant analogous scent.

mushroomy specific smell of some very old wines.

musky a difficult term: spicy/dusty, reminiscent of musk.

must unfermented grape juice.

musty due to poor casks or a cork fault. If the latter, allow the wine to stand after pouring and the smell may wear off after a few minutes.

neutral without positive flavour or marked physical characteristics. A common feature of many blended wines, from quite respectable commercial burgundy to litre-bottle carafe wine.

noble indicates stature and breed; a wine of towering elegance.

nose the broadest term for the bouquet, aroma, smell of a wine; the professional taster 'noses' a wine.

nuance having components reminiscent of specific smells, e.g. of almonds, of struck flint.

nutty a crisp rounded flavour associated with full-bodied dry white wines like Corton-Charlemagne, or good quality amontillados. Fine old tawny port has a distinct smell of cobnuts, hazels or brazil nuts.

oak an important factor, particularly in relation to fine wines. Oak casks impart an oaky, spicy, cinnamon taste and smell, desirable in moderation, undesirable if exaggerated.

objective relating to the object, measurable, factual.

off-taste unclean, tainted or diseased wine; though not necessarily undrinkable.

old can be a factual statement or imply a state of bouquet and taste adversely affected by overmaturity. Lacking freshness.

olfactory to do with the sense of smell and its perception.

ordinary in wine terms is mildly derogatory: a wine of no pretensions or with little merit.

organoleptic the testing, by use of the senses, in an analytical context, of wine and food.

oxidized flat, stale off-taste due to exposure to air.

peach-like self-descriptive. Characteristic of the bouquet of certain German wines, notably ripe wines from the Ruwer.

peardrops an undesirable overtone sometimes noticeable in poorly made white wines of lesser vintages. Wine probably unstable and in dubious condition, but may be quite drinkable.

penetrating powerful, with almost a physical effect on the nostrils. Almost certainly high in alcohol and volatile esters.

peppery a sort of raw harshness, rather hard to define, due to immature and unsettled components which have not had time to marry. Noticeable on young ruby and vintage port and many full young red wines. Probably higher alcohols.

perfume an agreeable scented quality of bouquet.

persistence length of flavour and of bouquet.

petrol analogous smell, slightly oily, petroleum overtone. Not necessarily bad.

pine related to turpentine. Breezy scent; quality Médocs.

piquant fresh and mouth-watering acidity. A desirable and customary feature of wines from the Mosel, Saar and Ruwer and from other districts, like Sancerre. Less desirable but not necessarily unattractive in other youthful red and white table wines with a little more acidity than expected or warranted.

plummy a red wine colour indicating neither youth nor maturity, in between, lacking clear definition.

poor not off or bad, but of no merit, character or quality.

positive marked, noticeable and notable, as opposed to little and dumb.

powerful self-explanatory, but more appropriately used in the context of a big red wine.

pricked an unpleasant sharpness due to excess volatile acidity. A pricked wine will not be pleasant to drink and will be beyond treatment. It may *just* be drinkable for it might not have reached the final vinegary stage.

prickly indicates on nose, but particularly on the palate, a sharp-edged, raw, possibly almost effervescent quality. Only tolerable in certain circumstances: raw, young vinho verde and similar *pétillant* wines.

puckering, mouth- a tactile sensation induced by high tannin content.

pungent powerful, assertive, heavily scented, spicy, often indicating a high degree of volatile acidity, as in old madeira.

quality three senses: quality wine, like fine wine, can be a vague and general term, often abused. In the EEC 'quality' wines are legally defined, with statutory minimum criteria. In the abstract sense, a wine exhibits quality by virtue of its correctness, refinement and clarity of colour; its pure varietal aroma or harmonious overtones of bouquet; with all its components well balanced, with rich and complex flavour, long finish and fragrant aftertaste.

racy an abstract term indicating zest, liveliness, breed.

raspberries a pleasant zestful and fairly common wine aroma, for example, a good Bourgueil (red Loire), some young beaujolais.

refreshing pleasant, thirst-quenching acidity.

resinous literally imparted by the addition of resin, mainly to Greek table wines. A very old practice but something of an acquired taste.

rich self-explanatory. Should not automatically imply sweetness, rather a full *ensemble* of fruit, flavour, alcohol and extract.

ripe wine in full bloom, having reached its maturity plateau. A mellowness prior to its decline. Ripe grapes give a wine a natural sweetness and richness.

robust full-bodied, tough yet rounded. A good strapping mouthful of wine. Could apply equally to a 13.5° Châteauneuf-du-Pape, Taylor '48 or La Mission Haut-Brion '75.

rough a coarse, edgy sort of wine, usually of ordinary quality.

round a feature of a well-balanced, usually mature, wine. No raw immature edges.

rubbery probably presence of mercaptan, a disagreeable accident of complex chemical background, not infrequently seen on old white wines due to the breakdown of sulphur.

rugged big, masculine, high in alcohol, over tannic.

salty one of the so-called four primary tastes, but perhaps the least applicable to wine. A self-descriptive tang characteristic of good fresh manzanilla.

sap the little-used equivalent of a somewhat enigmatic French term implying the quality of inherent life that will develop a fine young wine.

savoury rich, spicy; lip-smacking flavouriness.

scented agreeable, positive, grapey-flowery, high-toned aroma.

sensuous rich, smooth, opulent flavour and texture.

severe hard, unyielding and probably immature.

sharp a degree of acidity between piquant and pricked. Implies a stage beyond that of being attractively refreshing. It could, however, become mollified with bottle-age.

short refers to the length of flavour on the palate, abruptness, indicating lack of quality.

sick diseased, out of condition.

silky a firm yet distinctly soft texture on the palate. A characteristic of most really fine dessert wines, also of good quality Pomerols.

simple better than ordinary. Straightforward, un-complex.

sinewy lean yet muscular.

smoky a subtle overtone characteristic of some grapes in certain white wine districts, e.g. good oaky *chardonnay*.

smooth soft, easy texture. No rough edges.

soft self-descriptive. Mainly in reference to red wines. Mellow; tannin and acidity fully married and absorbed.

solid full-bodied, foursquare, packed with alcohol, tannin and acidity. Possibly somewhat undeveloped.

sorbic acid not a natural grape acid but one sometimes added as a preservative. Its presence can be detected by a faint garlic-like odour.

sound the first thing a wine should be: appearance clear and bright; wholesome, clean bouquet and flavour.

sour a term to be used with care. To the English, sour has an off-taste, overacid connotation. Others use the word as a synonym for natural, somewhat tart, acidity.

sparkling a wine containing an induced degree of efffer-vescence – the basis and whole point of a certain class of wine, such as champagne, the sparkle being obtained by the con-trolled release of carbon dioxide when the bottle is opened.

spicy a rich, herb-like aroma and flavour bestowed by certain grape varieties such as *gewürztraminer*; also derived from use of new oak casks. *See* CINNAMON.

spritz or **spritzig** a slight prickle often noted visually by small beads or bubbles at the rim and on the tongue, indicating a touch of carbonic acid gas usually induced or, in a very young acid wine, left by the wine-maker as a refreshing element in the wine. Examples abound: just a touch in some young mosels, blatant in vinho verde.

stalky reminiscent of the smell of damp twigs; a damp *chai*-like smell. This stalky or stemmy aroma is detectable in young wines and can arise from overprolonged contact with grape stalks during wine-making.

steely a firm, lean though not thin, white wine with a fair amount of acidity. For example, a good chablis or Puligny-Montrachet.

stewed a somewhat ill-defined nose, not clearly varietal, not clear cut and not as good as it should be. Possibly a heavily chaptalized wine.

stimulus that which provokes a sensory response.

stout high tannin associated with less high acidity and mellowness.

strange untypical, having a foreign smell or taste.

stringy skinnier than sinewy, not very well constructed.

strong powerful, alcoholic.

sturdy fairly tough, substantial.

suave soft, supple and harmonious.

subjective personal reaction, mental rather than measurable.

subtle veiled richness, unobvious complexity.

sugar grapes contain natural sugars which are converted through fermentation into alcohol. Traces of residual sugar in ripe wines are a major factor in the wine's evolution.

sugared/sugary several connotations: the sweet smell and blandness of a chaptalized wine; high sucrose content of a rich dessert wine.

sulphury sulphur, in its various forms, not only has a very pronounced volcanic smell but its presence can be detected physically by a prickly sensation in the nostrils and the back of the throat, like a whiff from a sulphur match or coke oven. It is commonly used as an antiseptic, for cleaning casks (by burning sulphur sticks) and bottles (using a mild sulphur dioxide solution) and if carelessly used or overused its undesirable odour will be retained. The bouquet of many young wines is masked by a whiff of sulphur which is quite harmless and often wears off a short while after the wine has been poured out.

superficial shallow, without depth or follow-through.

supple easy to taste and sense, hard to define. A combination of sap, vigour and amenable texture.

sweaty saddle a rudely evocative smell characteristic of certain Australian red wines made from *shiraz* grapes.

sweet a wine with a high sugar content, natural or contrived. The essential characteristic of any dessert wine. There are two types of sweetness; that which is merely sweet and the other which is from the richness of fine, well-ripened grapes. The former kind will always remain sweet (e.g. Pedro Ximenez sherry), the latter will dry out as it ages. Fine Rhine wines and sauternes can be recognized by the smell emanating from *pourriture noble*, but even dry wines can have a 'sweet', honeyed or grapey sweetness on the nose. The principal sweetening elements are fructose, sucrose, glucose; also, but less sweet, glycerol and alcohol.

sweetness is detected fleetingly on the tip of the tongue, on entry.

syrupy usually used in connection with an excessively rich, ripe sauternes, *Trockenbeerenauslese* or sweet sherry.

tactile that which provokes a response which can be physically felt (touched), e.g. sulphur, effervescence, velvety, creamy, burning (alcohol).

tang, tangy rich, high-toned, zestful bouquet and end-taste of an old madeira, old sherry, Tokay.

tannin an essential preservative derived from grape skins during fermentation. Part of the maturation process consists of the breaking down of the tannin content; it is precipitated over a period by the action of proteins and becomes, with colouring matter, part of the deposit or crust left in the bottle. The presence of tannin dries the roof of the mouth, grips the teeth and sometimes has a sweaty, leathery, dusty cellar smell. It is a particularly noticeable physical component of young red wine (bordeaux in particular) which has a practical purpose: to 'cut' fatty foods and clean the palate. Tannin is less of a factor in white wines as grape skins – the main source – are removed prior to fermentation. Tannin tends to mask the fruit aroma.

tart sharp and tongue-curling due to overacidity, often with a touch too much tannin. This condition can be due to premature harvesting of grapes or a late bad harvest. The wine could recover and soften; it may, on the other hand, disintegrate. More pronounced than piquant.

tartaric acid one of the good and essential acids in wine.

Tartaric acid in the form of free acidity or acid tartrate of potassium is widely distributed in the vegetable kingdom but its chief source is the grape. Its presence gives wine its healthy refreshing tang and contributes greatly to its liveliness, quality and crisp finish. Occasionally it can be seen as light white flakes precipitated in white wine and sherry which have been subjected to an unusually low temperature.

taut somewhat severe, probably immature, firm, unyielding.

thin deficient in natural properties; watery, lacking body.

threshold level at which a given smell or taste can be perceived. Thresholds vary from person to person, from substance to substance. It is possible with practice to lower (improve) olfactory and gustatory thresholds.

tough a full-bodied wine of overpowering immaturity (not necessarily young) with an excess of tannin. May well turn out in time to be a great wine.

twiggy like stalky and stemmy, mildly derogatory and usually relating to somewhat coarse young wines. A fine mature claret would never be described as twiggy. A raw young minor claret could.

unbalanced components ill-matched: overtannic, overacid, lacking fruit, etc.

unripe immature, raw; green; malic acidity of wine made from grapes not fully ripened.

vanilla a tannic-like compound derived from oak giving certain cask-aged wines a distinctive aroma. The principal smell of oak is derived from ethyl vanilline.

varietal a varietal aroma is one with the distinctive smell of a particular grape variety such as *cabernet sauvignon*. As a wine matures, its varietal aroma decreases as its bouquet develops.

vegetal hard to define. A flavour and character more root-like than herbaceous or flowery.

velvety a textural connotation, related to silky and smooth, but implying more opulence.

vigorous lively, healthy, positive flavour associated with youthful development.

vinegar the smell of ethyl acetate, one of the simple esters, indicative of bacteriological infection. The wine will be unfit to drink, acetic and beyond redemption.

vinosity having firm, well-constituted, vinous character and strength.

vinous a pleasant enough and positive winey smell or taste.

viscous heavy oily wine, detected visually by its clinging meniscus, pronounced legs, and texture on the palate.

volatile acidity this is present to a greater or lesser extent in all wine, but an excess is undesirable and often indicates the first step in acetic deterioration (*see* VINEGAR).

watery lacking fruit, extract, low in alcohol and acidity.

weak low in alcohol, feeble fruit and character.

weight the heaviness or lightness depending mainly on the alcohol and extract and can vary enormously with different types of wine, grape, area of origin, climate, etc. Light wines tend to be made in the more northerly regions, heavier (table) wines in hot southerly areas. For example, the light, low in alcohol, mosels and the heavier reds of the southern Rhône or the Cape; and compare the light red, white and rosé wines of the Loire with heavier fortified wines.

well balanced a satisfactory blend of physical components: fruit, acid, tannin, alcohol, etc., and, to a lesser extent, of the intangible elements: breed, character, finesse.

wishy-washy lacking crispness and distinctive flavour; neither here nor there.

withered usually in reference to an old, dried-out wine, losing fruit and flesh with age.

wood distinct and desirable odour derived from ageing in oak casks (*see also* VANILLA).

woody an undesirable taste imparted by wine kept too long in cask, or in unclean casks.

yeasty descriptive smell of ferments, live or dead. If detected in bottled wine, a sure indication of impending or recent secondary fermentation.

young, youthful a positive attractive feature: fresh, with youthful acidity; immature.

zest, zestful a lively, crisply flavoured wine.

zing exciting, refreshing attribute.

FRENCH TASTING TERMS

acerbe acid; excessively sharp and bitter.

âcre harsh.

agressif raw, unripe, unharmonious.

aigre sour, vinegary, acetic acid taste.

aimable agreeable, nicely balanced.

amer, amertume bitter, disagreeable.

américain, goût fairly sweet (in relation to champagne). More vulgarly, implies a sugared-up blend of wine for the American market.

anglais, goût this depends on the district and context. In champagne, dry; in burgundy, big and smooth.

âpre rough, harsh; high tannin content.

arôme aroma, relating to the perceived qualities arising from a particular grape variety, and so forth.

arrière-goût aftertaste.

asescence a bacteria-caused disease causing overacidity, leading to vinegar.

astringent astringent, tannic, mouth-puckering.

bois, goût de woody taste, often the result of wine stored too long in a new cask.

bouchonné cork-tainted; smell of cork.

bouquet scent or perfume of a developing or mature wine.

bourru, vin new wine showing cloudiness prior to falling bright.

brut very dry (in relation to champagne, minimum liqueuring).

capiteux heady, high in alcohol.

casse showing cloudiness or darkening of colour usually due to metallic contamination.

charnu fleshy; full-bodied but with good acidity.

chaud warm, alcoholic.

chemise coating – deposit on sides of bottle of old red wine.

chêne oaky character from the wood.

clairet light red, almost rosé.

classe wine of quality or potential.

complet balanced and harmonious.

corps body, robustness.

corsé full-bodied, well constituted. Satisfactory but probably not mature in that state.

coulant pleasant, easy to drink.

coupé cut, i.e. blended or diluted.

court short, lacking balance.

crémant creaming; slight sparkle.

creux hollow; momentary thinness on palate.

cuit, goût de wine with a cooked flavour, or with a natural flavour resulting from a hot summer, or very hot soil.

cuit, vin cooked flavour derived from addition of concentrated must.

dégustation tasting – the subject of this book.

délicat delicate; light consistency, usually low in alcohol.

demi-sec half-dry (in practice medium-sweet).

doux sweet.

dur hard; excess of tannin.

élégant elegant, stylish.

équilibré well-balanced, harmonious.

étoffé well-marked qualities and well conserved.

évent, goût d' nasty, unclean smell and flat taste.

éventé wine which has been abruptly overoxidized.

faible weak, thin.

ferme firm; the dumb unreadiness of a fine young wine.

ferment, goût de taste of a wine still fermenting; or in bottle having recently undergone a secondary fermentation; yeasty.

fin fine.

finesse grace, delicacy, breed, distinction.

fort strong.

frais fresh. In another context, cool.

franc natural, clean, sound.

français, goût sweet, particularly in relation to champagne.

fruité fruity.

fumet marked bouquet.

fusil, pierre à bouquet and/or taste reminiscent of gunflint.

garde, vin de good enough to lay down, or which *should* be laid down to mature.

généreux forthcoming; rich in body and extract.

goudron, goût de tarry taste.

goût taste. A term always qualified.

grain character; completeness.

graisse a diseased wine which is flat, faded and oily.

grossier big and coarse.

léger light in body and style.

liquoreux sweet and rich, implying a natural state.

long lingering flavour, intense and aromatic.

lourd heavy, dull, unbalanced.

mâché mashed: a disturbed, tired or unsettled wine.

maderisé maderized.

maigre meagre, thin and feeble.

mauvais goût bad taste; unfit to drink.

moelleux soft and rich, yet not necessarily sweet.

moisi, goût de taste of decay.

mou flabby, flat, lacking in character.

mouillé watered.

mousse froth, foam, sparkle.

mousseux sparkling (fully, like champagne).

mout unfermented grape juice.

mûr balanced, in a mature not a youthful context.

muté muted; a must whose fermentation has been artificially arrested (leaving an unusually high unfermented sugar content).

nature, vin natural unsugared wine.

nerveux firm, vigorous, vital; fine and well knit.

odeur smell, in the simple direct sense: smell of cork, smell of wine, of yeast.

oeil de perdrix 'partridge eye'; descriptive of the tawny-gold of certain types of wine.

onctueux full-bodied, fat and rich. Usually applies to sweet wines but not necessarily to the exclusion of red.

paille, goût de reminiscent of damp straw.

parfum perfume; fragrance. Term for grape aroma.

passé too old; going downhill (but may be drinkable, just).

pâteux thick, pasty consistency.

pauvre poor, small.

pelure d'oignon the colour of onion skin. May apply to certain *vin gris* and some rosé wines; occasionally to old and maderized white wines.

perlant slight sparkle more akin to a prickle (similar to the German term *spritzig*).

pétillant light natural sparkle.

petit a little wine, probably deficient in alcohol.

piquant sharp and acid; may be an attractive tartness or purely derogatory, depending on context.

piqué pricked. Dangerous degree of volatile acidity in a wine on its death-bed.

piqûre a disease which creates a grey film on the surface of the wine, decomposing the alcohol into vinegar.

plat flat and dull.

plein full. Not just body but character.

précoce precocious; early maturing.

race breed.

rancio, goût de smell characteristic of old *vin doux*. Usually involves a degree of oxidation; and is something of an acquired taste.

riche generous.

robe colour; generally used in relation to that of a fine wine.

rond, rondeur round, harmonious.

rude astringent.

sauvage, goût foxy taste imparted by native American vines and some hybrids.

saveur taste, in the mouth, in its broadest sense.

sec dry, fermented out.

séché dried out; harsh and flat. Withered after lying ullaged in bottle or too long in cask.

sève sap: a combination of vigour, firmness of body and aromatic persistence. The English have no equivalent term.

solide substantial, full-bodied but well balanced.

souple supple: no sharp edges; elegant balance, soft and pleasant to drink.

soyeux silky texture; supple, slightly plump.

spiritueux high in alcohol.

suave soft, supple, harmonious.

sucré a sweetness generally associated with arrested fermentation or some other less natural (i.e. added) degree of sugar.

taille, goût de raw, poor quality (after name for last pressing – the tail end).

tendre youthful delicacy. Charming: easy to drink; light and supple.

terne dull; lacking quality and interest.

terroir, goût de earthy smell and flavour derived from certain soils.

tourne a bacteriological disease that gives wine a dull appearance, a mousey smell and makes it flat yet acetic.

troublé troubled (appearance): hazy, cloudy. Wine diseased, or temporarily out of condition.

tuilé of tile-red colour. A curious stage that a wine might reach having lost its youthful purple hue, showing a maturity which may not be long-lived.

usé worn out; past best and on decline.

velouté velvety texture.

vert green – unripe.

vif fresh, young and lively.

vineux having vinosity; also high in alcohol.

vivace fresh and lively, implying youthful zing and possibly a certain tartness.

GERMAN TASTING TERMS

angereichert sugared.

ansprechend appealing; attractive.

art character.

artig smooth, rounded.

beerenton taste of (ripe) grapes.

bitter bitter.

bleichert rosé. Rare in Germany and mainly found in the Ahr valley, and Schillerwein.

blume bouquet.

blumig flowery; good.

bukettreich rich bouquet.

charaktervoll characterful.

delikat delicate.

duft fragrance.

edel noble, fine.

edelwein very fine.

elegant elegant, stylish.

erdig earthy.

fade insipid.

faul mouldy.

fein, feine fine.

feinste finest.

fett fat.

feunig high in alcohol.

firn maderized.

flüchtig little to it.

frisch fresh.

fruchtig fruity.

fülle full, rich.

gefällig pleasing and harmonious.

gering poorish.

gewürz spice: spiciness – of bouquet or flavour.

gezuckert sugared.

glatt smooth.

grosse great, big.

grün green; unripe.

gut good.

hart hard and tart.

hefegeschmack yeasty taste.

herb bitter.

hochfeine very fine.

holzgeschmack woody taste.

honigartig honeyed.

hübsch handsome, pretty; nice, at least.

jung young.

kernig firm.

körper body.

körperarm lacking body.

kräftig robust.
lebendig racy.
leer weak in character.
lieblich pleasant.
mager thin; lacking body.
mandelbitter bitter-almond flavour.
matt flat.
milde pleasantly soft, middle of the road.
naturrein, naturwein pure, unsugared.
nervig full-bodied.
oelig of marked viscosity.
perle light natural sparkle.
pikant intriguing in tangy, spicy sense.
rafle stemmy: harsh and green.
rassig showing race; breeding.
rauh raw.
reif ripe.
rein pure.
reintönig harmonious; well balanced.
rot red.
rund round, harmonious.
saftig juicy.
sauber pure; clean.
schal musty.
schaumwein sparkling wine.
schön lovely.
schwefel sulphur.
sehr fein very fine.
sekt sparkling wine.
spiel flexible, balanced.
spritzig with crisp natural prickle.
stahlig steely.
süffig not unlike *tendre* (French).
süss sweet.
trocken dry (in 'withered grape' sense).
ungezuckert unsugared; pure.
voll full.
vornehm exquisite, elegant, distinctive.
weinig vinous, displaying vinosity.
wuchtig potent.
würzig spicy.
zukunft for the future. A wine capable of development.

ITALIAN TASTING TERMS

abboccato with some sweetness.
acerbo taste of unripe apples.
aggressivo aggressive: raw, unripe, unharmonious.
allappante unpleasant, rough, ill-tempered.
amabile gentle, slightly sweet.
ammaccato disagreeable taste, between dry and musty.
ammandorlato blend of semisweet and almond-bitter tastes.
ampio ample: complete and generous.
aristocratico aristocratic; wine of fine pedigree: good soil, vines, vinification and vintage year.
armonico harmoniously blended and enhanced flavours.
asciutto dry: fermented out, clean.
aspro rough on the palate.
astringente astringent.
austero austere: a characteristic of big young wines.
carattere a wine of distinction and typical character.

FULL GLOSSARY OF TASTING TERMS

caratteristico with characteristic individual traits.
carrezzevole caressing: rich, flowing.
completo complete.
con retrogusto with aftertaste.
corpo body: rich in alcohol and extracts.
costituito well-constituted.
debole a wine with little character.
deciso with decisive qualities.
decrepito old and faded.
delicato fine and harmonious.
di corpo full-bodied; with high alcoholic degree.
duro hard, excess tannin.
elegante elegant, stylish.
equilibrato well balanced, harmonious.
erbaceo green, unripe, slightly piquant.
fiacco tired; lacking vigour.
franco blunt and straightforward. No subtleties.
fresco fresh in style, refreshing.
fruttato fruity.
generoso forthcoming; rich in body and extract.
grasso unctuous.
immaturo immature.
maderizzato o marsalato maderized.
magro lean; lacking body.
marca of marked character (of grape, type, district).
morbido tender, gentle, soft and caressing in the mouth.
nerbo lit. nerve. A wine of fibre and inner strength.
nervoso sensitive, delicate yet vivacious.
netto clean cut; basic taste particularly marked.
neutro neutral: of little character, lacking in acidity.
oleoso oily: probably spoiled.
passabile acceptable, inoffensive.
pieno full: with richness and body.
pronta beva a quickly maturing young wine.
rotondo round: full and mellow.
ruvido rough, raw-tasting.
salato salty character.
sapido similar to the French term *sève*.
secco dry: fermented out.
selvatico coarse, uncivilized character.
spogliato spoiled, through overageing.
stoffa applicable to great wines with mouth-filling, many-faceted qualities.
tannico tannic.
vellutado velvety texture.
verde green, unripe.
vinoso vinous.
vuoto empty: superficial, short flavoured.

_____ APPENDIX: _____
FOR FURTHER READING
AND INFORMATION

The following is a fairly comprehensive list of books written, mainly in English, on the subject of tasting, from the lightly instructive to the deeply academic. In this edition wine books of a general nature, whether discursive or factual, have been omitted, for to include them all would be tedious and confusing, and to select only those I rate highly would, I am afraid, offend a few friends and some literary acquaintances.

Some of these books are out of print so I list selected specialist wine book dealers who either stock, or can find, them; also some libraries that house major wine book collections.

I currently receive wine magazines and journals from all over the world so I have greatly extended this section, including only those, however, which regularly feature tasting notes.

There is nothing to beat tasting itself, for practice and experience cannot be swotted up from books. The only short cut I recommend is to attend a well-organized wine course with competent tutors. This appendix ends with some useful addresses.

The availability of paperback editions is indicated by †.

——— The scientific approach to tasting ———

Modern Sensory Methods of Evaluating Wines by M. A. Amerine, E. B. Roessler and F. Filipello (Hilgardia, University of California, June 1959). A scholarly pamphlet dealing with the senses, chemical components, statistical tasting techniques and mathematical scoring systems. One of the first modern treatises on the organoleptic examination of wine. Not for amateurs, even if they managed to obtain a copy.

Sensory Evaluation of Wines by M. A. Amerine and E. B. Roessler (Wine Institute, San Francisco, 1964). A follow-up of _Modern Sensory Methods_ but still concerned with the academic approach to product-testing.

Wines, Their Sensory Evaluation by Maynard A. Amerine and Edward B. Roessler (W. H. Freeman & Company, New York and Oxford, 1976; revised and enlarged 1983). Putting 'Wines' first, introducing the Christian names of the authors and including an odd _New Yorker_ cartoon or two is a clear indication of intent: to present two distinguished professors in assimilable form. However, whereas at least half the book is still too complex for non-academics, the remainder is a must. Though some curious prejudices are exhibited, it is scholarly, informative and impressive.

——————————— On the senses ———————————

Odour Description and Odour Classification by R. Harper, E. C. Bate-Smith and D. G. Land (J. and A. Churchill, London, 1968). Very scientific review of sytems and classifications.

Gustation and Olfaction edited by G. Ohloff and A. F. Thomas (Academic Press, London and New York, 1971). The proceedings of an international symposium sponsored by Firmenich et Cie, Geneva.

The Human Senses in Action by Roland Harper (Churchill Livingstone, Edinburgh and London, 1972). The structure of sense organs, nature of stimuli, methods of measuring perception; with an exhaustive bibliography. Dr Harper, of Reading University, writes for fellow scientists; but really keen wine students might well find the book fascinating, as I did.

For wine buffs

The Flavour of Wine by Dr Max Lake (Jacaranda Press Pty. Ltd., Sydney, 1969†). An attractive, original and sometimes complex little book by an erudite Australian surgeon-cum-winery owner.

Start to Taste Wine by Max Lake (1984).

How to Test and Improve Your Wine Judging Ability by Irving H. Marcus (Wine Publications, Berkeley, California, 1972†). A small paperback by the former owner-editor of *Wines and Vines*. The first part compact and helpful, the second a potted version of the Amerine-Roessler evaluation tests.

Understanding Wine by Michael Schuster (Mitchell Beazley, 1989). Accurate, logical, attractively produced, highly recommended.

For beginners

Wine Taster's Secrets by Andrew Sharp (Horizon, Toronto, 1981†). Extremely unoriginal – as admitted by the author.

Masterglass by Jancis Robinson (Pan Books, 1983†). A sensible, 'jolly hockey-sticks' approach with unnecessarily complicated layout. However, effective, and recommended.

Lateral Wine-tasting by Rosemary George MW (Bloomsbury, 1991). Basic information, unoriginal. Clever but quirky. Mosel does not appear in the index (Nahe does) but alphabetically in the text alongside Bernkastel.

The Taste of Wine by Jill Goolden (BBC Books, 1990). Deals with table wines only and is as unoriginal as its title. Sound, though written in a cosy, journalistic style. On the other hand, its aim – to describe individual types of wine – is achieved pretty well.

The Wine Tasters Notebooks by Tom Stevenson (Stevenson, 1989).

Enjoying Wine, a Taster's Companion by Pamela Vandyke-Price (Heinemann, 1982).

In French

La Dégustation des Vins by Raymond Brunet (Bureau du Moniteur Vinicole, Paris, c. 1930).

Les Caractères du Vin by Raymond Brunet (Bureau du Moniteur Vinicole, Paris, c. 1935).

Le Physiologie du Goût by Brillat-Savarin (1825).

Le Goût (L'Amateur de Bordeaux Cahiers, 1992).

Le Goût Juste by Jacques Puisais (Flammarion, 1985).

In other languages
Danish

On at Smage på vin by Michael Broadbent, translated by Kay Nielsen (Chr. Erichsens Forlag, København, 1975).

Vinsmagning by Michael Broadbent, translated by Henning Albrechtsen (Chr. Erichsens Forlag, København, 1982).

Dutch

Vijn proeven by Michael Broadbent, translated by Diets van Vessem (Elsevier, Amsterdam, 1987).

German

Weine prüfen, kennen, geniessen by Michael Broadbent, translated by Hanspeter Reichmuth (Raeber, Luzern and Stuttgart, 1976, 1979, 1986 and 1990).
Broadbent's Weinnotizen (Hallwag, 1994).

Japanese

Wine tasting by Michael Broadbent, translated by Nobuko Nishioka (Tokyo, 1978, 1982, 1985 and 1990).

Spanish

Cómo se disfruta y se entiende la degustación del Vino by Michael Broadbent, translated by Ing Juan B. Morales Doria (Editorial Regina de los Angeles, S.A., Mexico City, 1981).
Guía para conocer y degustar Los Vinos by Michael Broadbent (Guias de bolsillo, Folio, Barcelona, 1982).

Swedish

Vinprovarens Handbok by Michael Broadbent, translated by Professor Nils Sternby (Norstedts Forlag, Stockholm, 1986).

─────────── **Translated for Americans** ───────────

Initiation into the Art of Wine Tasting by J. A. Vaccaro (Interpublish Inc, Madison, Wisconsin, 1974†). A rather laboured version of the *Précis . . .* by Puisais and Chabanon (opposite), well illustrated and interesting, but including the original irrelevant apple and cream-cracker score sheets and information about French hotel school courses.

─────────── **Books with tasting a major feature** ───────────

Notes on a Cellar-book by George Saintsbury (Macmillan, London, 1920). Detailed reminiscent jottings, which had a seminal influence on wine writing and connoisseurship (new edition with Yoxall preface, 1979).
The Physiology of Taste by Brillat-Savarin (Peter Davies, London, 1925†). A famous classic: discursive, civilized. Translated from the French *Physiologie du Goût*, 1825.
A Matter of Taste, Wine and Wine Tasting by Jack Durac (André Deutsch, London, 1975). Also published as *Wines and the Art of Tasting* (Sunrise, E. P. Dutton and Co. Inc, New York, 1974). A New York book reviewer incorrectly credited Mr Durac, a research scientist at London University, with being 'the first' to make 'a systematic attempt at explaining how a wine should be tasted . . .' etc. Appalling maps, stodgy production, some curious approaches, but full of earnest guidance.
The Taste of Wine by Pamela Vandyke-Price (Macdonald and Jane's, London, 1975). Sixty pages of somewhat idiosyncratic taste classifications flanked by less original general matter: wine making, maps and so forth. This book outlines the tasting approach of one professional writer. But there are other methods if this approach is not for you. Nevertheless, this book contains a broad spectrum of information.
Gorman on Californian Premium Wines by Robert Gorman (Ten Speed Press, Berkeley, California, 1975†). Thoughtful approach to tasting, with model notes.
The Great Vintage Wine Book II by Michael Broadbent (Mitchell Beazley, London, and Knopf, New York, 1991). A complete record of vintages of all the major classic districts, good, bad and indifferent, and the reasons why, illustrated with 5000 tasting notes.
Harry Waugh's Wine Diaries (Christie's Wine Publications). A series of travel journals and notes on tastings that started with

Bacchus on the Wing, *The Changing Face of Wine* and *The Pick of the Bunch* (all Wine & Spirit Publications, London, 1966, 1968 and 1970); *Diary of a Wine Taster* and *Winetaster's Choice* (both Quadrangle, New York, 1972 and 1973) and *Harry Waugh's Wine Diary Volumes Six, Seven, Eight and Nine* (Christie's Wine Publications, 1975, 1976, 1978 and 1981†). Personal, full of warmth, charm, enthusiasm and honestly expressed opinions on wines and vintages.

Académie du Vin Wine Course by Steven Spurrier and Michel Dovaz (Century Publishing in association with Christie's, London, 1983). The complete study course in wine appreciation of the Académie du Vin, Paris. Recommended.

The Taste of Wine by Emile Peynaud (Macdonald, London, 1987). A conscientious translation by Michael Schuster of the original 1980 French version. Recommended.

───────────── **Wine libraries** ─────────────

The Guildhall Library, in the City of London, houses the Library of the Institute of Masters of Wine, which in turn incorporates the old Wine Trade Club Library, founded and amassed by André Simon (Reference library open to the public).

The Jack Harvey Memorial Library, forming part of the Harvey Wine Museum in Bristol (well worth a *détour*, but by appointment only).

The Fresno State College Wine Library, California, incorporating the extensive library collected by Roy Brady, a former editor of *Wine World*.

The A. J. Winkler Library in the department of Viticulture and Enology, University of California, Davis.

Public Libraries: most public libraries in the United Kingdom have a food and wine section, and titles not stocked can usually be obtained, on request, through inter-library loans.

───────────── **Specialist wine booksellers** ─────────────

Janet Clarke, Antiquarian Books (3 Woodside Cottages, Freshford, Bath, BA3 6EJ).

Mrs Marion L. Gore (Box 433, San Gabriel, California 91775, USA).

M. M. Einhorn Maxwell, Books (At the Sign of the Dancing Bear, 80 East 11th Street, New York, NY 10003, USA).

Peter Willis (Newmarket House, Nailsworth, Gloucestershire, GL6 ORD). Permanent stock of prints and wine books. Also a print publisher.

The Wine & Food Library, Janice B. Longone (1207 West Madison, Ann Arbor, Michigan 48103, USA).

───────────── **Wine magazines** ─────────────

Decanter (Priory House, 8 Battersea Park Road, London SW8 4BG). The best English monthly.

Wine (Thames House, 5–6 Church Street, Twickenham, Middlesex, TW1 3NJ). Monthly. Lively, with regular tasting reports.

The Wine Spectator (387 Park Ave. South, New York, NY 10016 USA).

Food and Wine International (750 Third Avenue, New York, NY 10017, USA).

Quarterly Review of Wines (24 Garfield Ave. Winchester, MA 01890 USA).

Wine (2302 Perkins Place, Silver Spring, Maryland 10910,

USA). The Journal of the *Les Amis du Vin* organization of America.

Which? Wine Guide (14 Buckingham Street, London WC2). Notes and recommendations for consumers.

Wine Tidings (Suite 414, 5165 Sherbrooke St. West, Montreal, Quebec H4A 1T6, Canada).

La Revue du Vin de France (65 Montmartre, 75002 Paris, France). Five issues per annum. Old-established, high-grade.

Le Nouveau Guide Gault-Millau (210 Faubourg St-Antoine, 75012 Paris, France). Stimulating, often provocative, always lively *critique* of food, wine and restaurants.

Cuisine & Vins de France (11 avenue de l'Opéra, 75001 Paris, France).

Wine & Spirit Buying Guide (P.O. Box 113, Lane Cove 2066, Australia).

Winestate (80 Pirie Street, Adelaide, South Australia 5000). Authoritative monthly. Articles on wine, areas, personalities. Full coverage of new releases.

Wineglass (Wineglass Publishing Ltd., P.O. Box 9527, Newmarket, Auckland, New Zealand).

Vinum (Klosbachstrasse 83, Postfach 8030 Zürich, Switzerland). German language. Monthly. Excellent.

Wijn & Spijs (Kleiweg 13, 1396 HV Baambrugge, Abcoude, Netherlands).

Falstaff Magazin (Opernringhof, Opernring 1, Stiege E, 1 Stock, A-1010 Vienna, Austria). Monthly.

Gourmet, das Internationale Magazin Für Gutes Essen The only hardback glossy quarterly. Outstanding quality.

Vini (Via Sudorno 44, 24100 Bergamo Alta, Italy). A glossy and lively wine and food monthly.

Alles über Weine (Woschek Verlag, Wilhelm-Theodor-Römheld-Strasse 30, D-6500 Mainz, Germany). The best German monthly.

Arnes Journal (Arne Krüger GmbH, K.G., Wintergasse 4, 6203 Hochheim, West Germany). Monthly.

L'Ettichetta Superbly produced Italian quarterly.

Subscription wine newsletters

The Vine (2 Sunderland Road, London W5 4JY). Clive Coates' in-depth reports and tasting notes.

The Wine Advocate (1002 Hillside View, Parkton, Maryland 21120, USA). Robert Parker Jr's highly confident, influential and competent bi-monthly tasting notes.

Wine courses/Academies

Vini-viticultural schools, sometimes departments of universities, have for many years existed in major wine-producing countries: Geisenheim in Germany, Roseworthy in Australia, Montpellier in France; at the University of California, Davis and at the University of Bordeaux, to mention just a few.

The following establishments run regular structured courses open to all; in the listing they are followed by some of the firms and organizations which specialize in one-off tutored tastings. Their effectiveness depends partly on the class of wine and quality of individual tutors. Naturally these vary, but I venture to suggest that the overall level is surprisingly high and keen amateurs as well as beginners will certainly gain a lot from attending them.

Christie's Wine Course in association with L'Académie du Vin

(63 Old Brompton Road, London SW7 3JS). Regular evening courses from introductory to advanced.

Sotheby's (34 New Bond Street, London W1). Lecture/tastings.

Wine & Spirit Education Trust Ltd., London (Five Kings House, 1 Queen Street Place, London EC4R 1QS). Day and evening courses for the trade but open to all. Three levels: elementary, intermediate and advanced (for Diploma).

Wine & Spirit Education Centers of America Inc., Atlanta (Frank H. Stone, P.O. Box 20450, Atlanta, Georgia 30325, USA). Operates with franchises of Wine & Spirit Education Trust (UK).

International Wine Center, New York (144 West 55 Street, New York, NY 10019, USA). Regular classes. Wine bar below lecture/tasting rooms.

Windows On The World Wine School, New York (Windows On The World Restaurant, One World Trade Center, 107th Floor, New York, NY 10048, USA). Quite long-established and highly regarded.

'Wine Captain's Seminar', New York (The Sommelier Society of America, 435 Fifth Avenue, New York, NY 10016, USA).

Independent Wine Education Guild, Canada (A.C. Hirons, P.O. Box 883, Station Q, Toronto, Ontario, Canada, M4T 2N7).

KWV Wine Courses, South Africa (Laborie Wine Centre, P.O. Box 528, Suider Paarl 7624).

Centre d'Information, de Documentation et de Dégustation, Paris (45, rue Liancourt, 75104 Paris, France). Evening courses.

Ecole du Vin, Bordeaux (Château Loudenne, Saint-Yzans du Médoc, 33340 Lesparre, France). Residential courses.

Flemming Hvelplund's Wine School, Denmark (Magstrade 7, 1207 Copenhagen, Denmark). Effective, open to all.

German Wine Academy, at Kloster Eberbach (details from the German Wine Information Centre, 121 Gloucester Place, London W1H 3PJ). There are six 5-day courses a year on German wines only.

Wijnacademie, Rijswijk (Postbus 1840, 2280 D.V. Rijswijk, Netherlands).

INDEX